MAIMONIDES' PRINCIPLES
The Fundamentals of Jewish Faith

י"ג עקרים של הרמב"ם

Aryeh Kaplan

Published by the National Conference of Synagogue Youth,
the youth movement of the Orthodox Union,
Eleven Broadway, New York, NY 10004.
212.563-4000. www.ou.org.

Distributed by Mesorah Publications, Inc., 4401 Second Avenue,
Brooklyn, NY 11232. Distributed in Israel by Sifriati/A. Gitler
Books, 4 Bilu Street, P.O.B. 14075, Tel Aviv 61140. Distributed in
Europe by J. Lehmann Hebrew Booksellers, 20 Cambridge Terrace,
Gateshead, Tyne & Wear, England NE8 1RP.

ISBN 1-879016-04-4

PRINTED IN THE UNITED STATES OF AMERICA

Contents

A Publication

in the

JOSEPH
TANENBAUM
LIBRARY
Series

Preface

by Rabbi Baruch Taub

The very formulation of a system of Jewish discipline is more profound than the discipline itself. In establishing the 13 Principles of Jewish Faith, Rambam (Rabbi Moses Maimonides) is stating that being Jewish itself is an obligation. In so doing, the myth of often repeated expressions such as "I am a Jew at heart" is put to rest. To be a "Jew at heart" requires the development of a sense of obligation to the heart of Jewishness. Rather than a "do your own thing" system defined by the individual Jew, being Jewish means individual articulation of the established 13 Principles of Faith.

In truth, it is the contemporary Jew himself who has put this myth to rest. We are experiencing what has been popularly termed a generation of *teshuva* (return). It is our contention that young Jews today have moved the "*teshuva* movement" to a new place of development. No longer are contemporary Jews interested in learning about Judaism. There is an eagerness to learn and live Judaism itself. There has been a demand of late for Jewish classical literature in the vernacular as opposed to books "about" Judaism, and the response has been a noble one. In recent years, the great works of traditional Jewish literature have been made available to the layman and have greatly advanced the cause of Torah and mitzvot. Being Jewish is now being approached by young Jews throughout the world with that sense of obligation which lies at the heart of Rambam's Principles of Jewish Faith. The challenge is to oblige this growing sense of obligation.

In this vein, it is instructive to note that RAVAD (Rabbi Abraham Ben David) takes issue with Rambam with regard to the third of the 13 Principles. This principle, according to Rambam, states that God has no bodily form.

Ravad insists that the non-corporeality of God is not to be considered as one of the 13 Principles of Jewish Faith. To be sure, Ravad's disagreement with Rambam is not based upon a contention that God in fact does exist in bodily form. Clearly, Ravad's concern is that the many anthropomorphic references of the Torah ("hand of God" etc.) will lead the unschooled layman to conclude that He in fact does embody human form. If this then was a fundamental principle of Jewish faith, contends Ravad, many unknowing laymen would be discouraged from living up to Jewish expectation. Ravad's concern therefore is that the spirit of Rambam's fundamental principles should open doors to the searching Jew rather than close them.

This popular version of the 13 Principles of Jewish Faith represents a summarized version of the original work which appears in Rambam's commentary to the *Mishna Sanhedrin*. In presenting the commentary to the popular version, Rabbi Kaplan draws upon the original work as well as other sources utilizing his extensive knowledge of Jewish sources.

This work is an effort to perpetuate what was undoubtedly the intent of Rambam in presenting these fundamentals. To open the doors of the storehouse of Torah living and learning for the unschooled, as well as to provide a keener understanding of the basic principles of Jewish responsibility to both schooled and unschooled alike, is at the heart of this presentation.

May its dissemination encourage increased sensitivity to the Torah way.

Introduction

One of the clearest statements of Jewish belief is that contained in Maimonides' Thirteen Principles of Faith. These were first enunciated in his commentary on the Mishnah and, in an abbreviated form, are found in virtually every prayer book. They also form the basis of the well known synagogue hymn, *Yigdal*.

In formulating these principles, Maimonides went through the entire length and breadth of Jewish literature, determining which principles are always taken for granted and are unique to Judaism. In clear, concise language, he then set these down in the well-known Thirteen Principles. These principles have been discussed for the past eight hundred years, and are still accepted by all Jews as the one clear unambiguous creed of Judaism.

For the Jew, however, it was never enough merely to accept a creed. One can believe, but if one does not act on the basis of his belief, then his statement of faith is just so many empty words. On the other hand, however, one cannot practice Judaism in any sense at all unless he understands and believes in the roots from which it stems.

It is important to know something about the compiler of these most important principles. Moses Maimonides is considered the greatest codifier and philosopher in Jewish history. He is often affectionately referred to as the Rambam, after the initials of his name and title, *Rabenu Moshe Ben Maimon* (Our Rabbi, Moses son of Maimon).

Moses Maimonides was born in the city of Cordova, Spain, on a Sabbath, the day before Passover (14 Nissan 4895, or March 30, 1135), at one o'clock in the afternoon. It is not often that the birth of an ancient Jewish sage is known with such minute accuracy. Usually, we do not even know the year, let alone the day and hour. But so great was his renown, even in his lifetime, that many of the most minute details of Maimonides' life remain preserved.

Maimonides was only thirteen when his native city of Cordova fell into the hands of the Almohades, fanatical zealots from Morocco, who renewed the ancient motto of the early Moslem conquerors, "The Koran or the Sword." Under their rule, no Jew dared openly avow his faith, and Maimonides and his family were forced to emigrate.

They wandered from city to city in Spain, and finally, in 1160, settled in Fez, Morocco. It was during these wanderings that Maimonides began working on the first of his major works, his Commentary on the Mishnah.

The Mishnah, the earliest portion of the Talmud, had been compiled almost a thousand years earlier by Rabbi Judah the Prince, and details of its development are outlined in detail in the Eighth Principle. Written in extremely concise language, the Mishnah formed the basis of all later Talmudic writings, but by itself, it was most difficult to understand. Maimonides wrote the first clear commentary on this work that was so central to Jewish thought.

It is most interesting to note that this Commentary was written in Arabic, the spoken language of most Mediterranean Jews, rather than in the more scholarly Hebrew. Maimonides was writing for his contemporaries, and was aware of the need to communicate in a language with which they were familiar.

It was in this commentary that Maimonides first enunciated the Thirteen Principles of Faith. In the tenth chapter of the tract of *Sanhedrin*, the Mishnah outlines the beliefs that are basic to Judaism. The Thirteen Principles are basically an elaboration of this Mishnah.

In this volume, we have attempted to present the Principles as they appear in this Commentary in clear, precise English. Whenever we refer to the "Commentary on Mishnah," our reference is to this first enunciation of these principles. We will also refer to other places in the Commentary on the same Mishnah, and will speak of it as "Commentary on Mishnah, *Sanhedrin* 10:1."

The Moslem persecutions finally caught up with Maimonides' family in Fez, and they left for Israel in 1165, where they lived briefly in Jerusalem and Hebron. Finding life in the Holy Land very difficult, they then moved to Egypt and settled in Fostat. Supporting himself as a jewelry merchant in partnership with his brother David, he spent every spare moment working on his Commentary to the Mishnah. It was finally completed in 1168, and was published under the Arabic title *Kitab as-Siraj*, meaning "Book of Illumination."

This work itself would have been enough to establish Maimonides' reputation as a giant of Jewish scholarship. It is included in every edition of the Talmud, and is considered the clearest explanation of the Mishnah ever written. Thus, at the age of 33, Maimonides attained a reputation as one of the leading rabbinical authorities in Egypt, and was soon appointed chief rabbi of Cairo and spiritual leader of all Egyptian Jewry. Besides this, Maimonides also established for himself a considerable reputation as a physician, and in 1170 was appointed physician to Saladin's grand visier, Alfadhil. Although occupied both as court physician and as healer to his own people, he still found time to embark upon another monumental project, the codification of all the laws of the Talmud.

Anyone who has ever studied Talmud is familiar with the *Gemorah*, the second and last part of the Talmud. Written as a commentary on the Mishnah, in many places it almost assumes the form of minutes of the debates which took place in the great Talmudic academies of Israel and Babylon. Many laws appear in the discussion in places where the main debate centers around a completely different topic. In order to determine a law, one must often track down every place it is mentioned in such debates. This is an extremely difficult task, even for a major Talmudic scholar. Remember, in size the Talmud is approximately the same as the *Encyclopedia Britannica*.

Maimonides spent twelve years extracting every decision and law from the Talmud, and arranging them all into 14 systematic volumes. The work was finally completed in 1180, and was called *Mishneh Torah*, or "Code of the Torah." It was also called the *Yad Chazakah* or "Strong Hand." The word *Yad* (hand) in Hebrew is written exactly the same as the number 14, alluding to the 14 volumes of this work. For short, it is often called the *Yad* or simply the "Rambam."

This code established Maimonides as the leading Jewish authority of his generation. In communities such as Spain it became as popular as the Bible, and virtually every family owned a copy. The author's name became a household word in Jewish communities throughout the world.

Although the Thirteen Principles are not discussed explicitly in this Code, they play an important role in a number of areas. This is particularly true of the first section, where the "Foundations of the Torah" are discussed, and later in the section on "Repentance," which speaks of man's condition in general.

Here again, we will bring the pertinent sections of the *Yad* in translation. In many places the style here is more concise and legalistic than in the Commentary on the Mishnah, and the discussion also often involves much greater detail. This is especially true when it involves the interpretation of one of the commandments of the Torah.

At the same time that Maimonides' reputation as a Torah giant was becoming established, he was also attaining renown as a physician. For almost a thousand years, the teachings of the Greek physician Galen were accepted without question, often with disastrous results. Maimonides was the first to challenge these teachings, and, on the basis of his own experiments, developed many new and radical cures. He became renowned for his ability to affect cures after all other doctors had given up hope, and in 1185 was appointed physician to the royal court of Saladin, the sultan of Egypt and Syria.

In this position, Maimonides soon became established as the greatest physician of his generation. His fame even spread to England, where Richard the Lion Hearted invited him to become his personal physician. The great sage and physician elected, however, to remain in Egypt.

During this period, Maimonides was involved in preparing his third major work. This was also written in Arabic, and was first published in 1190 under the title *Dalalat al Hairin*. It is better known by its Hebrew name, *Moreh Nevuchim* or "Guide to the Perplexed."

What Maimonides had done was to integrate all the philosophical knowledge of his time, and clearly demonstrate how it all blended in with the teachings of the Torah. This work firmly established Maimonides as the dean of all Jewish philosophers. It not only attained a reputation as the greatest work on Jewish philosophy ever written, but also gained a place among the great classics of world philosophy in general.

Although a considerable amount of the material in the *Guide* deals with the Thirteen Principles, much of it is presented in a manner almost unintelligible to the person not familiar with philosophical terminology. We therefore only bring a single quote from this monumental work, in our discussion of the Fourth Principle.

A fourth major work of Maimonides was his *Sefer HaMitzvos*, or "Book of Commandments," also written in Arabic, in which he clearly enumerates the 613 commandments of the Torah. Besides all this, he also found time to write books on both Medicine and Astronomy.

Maimonides thus achieved the highest eminence as a Talmudist, codifier, philosopher and physician. His accomplishments in any one of these fields would have been enough to assure him a prominent place in history. The fact that he was able to excell in all four fields established him as an individual unique in the annals of history.

Besides his major works, Maimonides also wrote a number of shorter letters and essays, mostly in Arabic. The most famous of these is his *Iggeres Taimon* or "Letter to Yemen," in which he offered his oppressed brethren encouragement and urged them not to despair.

Another important essay is his *Maamar Techiyas HaMesim* or "Discourse on the Resurrection," which was written in 1191. A short excerpt is included in the Thirteenth Principle.

Maimonides' strength began to fail him in his old age, and he died in his seventieth year on 20 Teveth, 4963 (December 13, 1204) in Fostat. He was mourned by Jews all over the world and eventually buried in Tiberias, where his grave is a shrine to this very day.

About a hundred years after Maimonides' death, Rabbi Daniel bar Yehudah of Rome made the Thirteen Principles into a song. It is known as *Yigdal*, and is included in all prayer books and sung in synagogues around the world.

In presenting Maimonides' writings in English, we are merely following his own example of expressing the truths of Judaism in a language readily accessible to the average man. We will also include a brief discussion guide after each principle, and it is hoped that this will further help make this volume a useful tool for classes and discussion groups.

It is most important that we recognize the central core of principles which the rest of the Torah serves to express. It was for this reason that the Thirteen Principles were originally set forth. In our generation, more than any time in the past, this is needed. We live in an age where we are constantly exposed to principles diametrically opposed to the Torah, and it is vital that we clarify for ourselves, and especially for those whose ignorance makes them vulnerable to confusion, the essential uniqueness of Torah thought.

May it be God's will that this volume make a small contribution in this direction.

Aryeh Kaplan
Rosh Chodesh Sivan, 5733

Translator's Note:
For the sake of clarity, it has occasionally been necessary to add words or phrases not included in the original text. All such additions are indicated by square brackets. The same is true of portions of Biblical verses absent in the original, but included in the translation.

Ar. K.

THE THIRTEEN PRINCIPLES

1. I believe with perfect faith that God is the Creator and Ruler of all things. He alone has made, does make, and will make all things.

2. I believe with perfect faith that God is One. There is no unity that is in any way like His. He alone is our God—He was, He is, and He will be.

3. I believe with perfect faith that God does not have a body. Physical concepts do not apply to Him. There is nothing what-soever that resembles Him at all.

4. I believe with perfect faith that God is first and last.

5. I believe with perfect faith that it is only proper to pray to God. One may not pray to anyone or anything else.

6. I believe with perfect faith that all the words of the prophets are true.

7. I believe with perfect faith that the prophecy of Moses is abso-lutely true. He was the chief of all prophets, both before and after him.

8. I believe with perfect faith that the entire Torah that we now have is that which was given to Moses.

9. I believe with perfect faith that this Torah will not be changed, and that there will never be another given by God.

10. I believe with perfect faith that God knows all of man's deeds and thoughts. It is thus written (*Psalm 33:15*), "He has molded every heart together, He understands what each one does."

11. I believe with perfect faith that God rewards those who keep His commandments, and punishes those who transgress Him.

12. I believe with perfect faith in the coming of the Messiah. How long it takes, I will await his coming every day.

13. I believe with perfect faith that the dead will be brought back to life when God wills it to happen.

YIGDAL

1.   Great is the living God, and praised
       He exists, yet His existence has no time.

2.   He is One, no unity is like His,
           He is hidden, His unity has no end.

3.   He does not have bodily form, He is not a body
       He is beyond compare in His holiness.

4.   He preceded all things that were created,
           He is first, yet without beginning.

5.   He is the Lord of the world, and all things created
       Display His greatness and His majesty.

6.   He has granted the bounty of His prophecy
           To the men of His choice and glory.

7.   There has not arisen another like Moses
       A prophet who looked upon His image.

8.   God gave a true Torah to His people,
           Through His prophet, trusted in all His house.

9.   God will not replace not change His Law
       For all time, for anything else.

10.   He sees, He knows our secrets,
          He see each thing's end at its very beginning.

11.   He rewards man with love, as his deeds deserve,
       He gives the wicked evil, according to their wrong.

12.   He will send our Messiah at the End of Days,
          To redeem those who await His final salvation.

13.   God will bring the dead to life with His great love,
       May His glorious name be blessed for all time.

בֶּאֱמוּנָה שְׁלֵמָה
שֶׁהַבּוֹרֵא, יִתְבָּרַךְ שְׁמוֹ,
הוּא בּוֹרֵא וּמַנְהִיג
לְכָל־הַבְּרוּאִים,
וְהוּא לְבַדּוֹ
עָשָׂה וְעוֹשֶׂה וְיַעֲשֶׂה
לְכָל־הַמַּעֲשִׂים.

The First Principle

I believe with perfect faith that God is the Creator and ruler of all things. He alone has made, does make, and will make all things.

Yigdal
Great is the Living God, and praised,
He exists, yet His existence has no time.

Commentary on Mishnah
The first principle involves belief in the existence of God.

There is a Being, perfect in every possible way, who is the ultimate Cause of all existence.

All existence depends on Him and is derived from Him.

It is inconceivable that He not exist. If He did not exist, everything else would also cease to exist and nothing would remain.

If, however, we could imagine that nothing else existed, He would not cease to exist. He would not be diminished in any way.

Only God is totally self-sufficient and, therefore, Unity and Mastery belong only to Him. He has everything that He needs in Himself and does not need anything else at all.

Everything else, however, whether it be an angel, a star, or anything associated with them above or below, all depend on Him for their very existence.

The Torah teaches us this first principle in the first of the Ten Commandments (*Exodus 20:2*): "I am the Lord your God."

Code, Foundations of the Torah
(Yad, Yesodey HaTorah)

1:1   The ultimate foundation and pillar of wisdom is the realization that there is a first Being who brought everything else into existence.

Everything else in heaven and earth only exists as a result of the reality of His existence.

1:2   If one could conceive that He did not exist, then neither could

13

anything else exist.

1:3 If, however, one could conceive that nothing else existed, then He alone would still exist.

He would not cease to exist when they did; for all things depend on Him, but He does not depend on them at all.

Therefore, nothing is quite as real as He is.

1:4 The Prophet therefore said (*Jeremiah 10:10*), "The Lord, God, is Real." Only He is real. Nothing else is real in the sense that He is.

The Torah likewise says (*Deuteronomy 4:35*), "There is nothing else besides Him." Nothing else shares His ultimate reality.

1:5 This Being is God of the world, Lord of all the earth...His power has neither end nor limit...

1:6 To know this is one of the commandments of the Torah. It is thus written (*Exodus 20:2*), "I am the Lord your God."

Code, Repentance
(Yad, Tshuvah)

3:7 Five are in the category of the nonbeliever (*Min*): One who says that there is no God and that the world has no Master...

Points for Discussion

1. How do we define God?

2. Why do we say that God is both Creator and Ruler? Is it possible that He be one without being the other? Are there religions or philosophies that only believe in one of these two facets?

3. What do we mean when we say that God is perfect in every possible way?

4. We say that God does not need His creation. If so, why did He create the world? What do we say of a person when he does something that he is not required to do? How does this relate to God?

5. What do we mean when we say that nothing is as real as God?

6. The first of the Ten Commandments reads, "I am the Lord your God, who took you out of the land of Egypt, from the house of slavery." Why is the Exodus mentioned in this commandment, and not creation itself? That is, why does the first commandment not say, "I am the Lord your God, who created you?"

7. Maimonides (Rambam) counts "I am the Lord" as a commandment to believe in God. How is it possible for God to command us to believe in Him? What purpose does this commandment serve?

8. Nachmanides (Ramban) disputes Maimonides and contends that belief in God is the foundation of our faith and therefore cannot be considered a mere commandment. Discuss both opinions.

9. Discuss the verse in *Yigdal* in light of this principle. Is time also included among the things that depend on God?

אֲנִי מַאֲמִין

בֶּאֱמוּנָה שְׁלֵמָה
שֶׁהַבּוֹרֵא, יִתְבָּרַךְ שְׁמוֹ,
הוּא יָחִיד,
וְאֵין יְחִידוּת כָּמוֹהוּ
בְּשׁוּם פָּנִים,
וְהוּא לְבַדּוֹ אֱלֹהֵינוּ,
הָיָה, הֹוֶה, וְיִהְיֶה.

The Second Principle

I believe with perfect faith that God is One. There is no unity that is in any way like His. He alone is our God—He was, He is, and He will be.

Yigdal
He is One, no unity is like His,
He is hidden, His unity has no end.

Commentary on Mishnah
The second principle involves the unity of God. We believe that the Cause of everything is One.

He is not one, however, like a member of a pair or species.

He is furthermore not like a single thing, which can be divided into a number of elements.

He is not even like the simplest physical thing, which is still infinitely divisible.

God is One in a unique way. There is no other unity like His.

The Torah teaches us this second principle when it says (*Deuteronomy 6:4*), "Hear O Israel, the Lord is our God, the Lord is One."

Code, Foundations of the Torah
(Yad, Yesodey HaTorah)
1:6 If one even allows himself to think that there is another deity other than God, then he violates the commandment (*Exodus 20:3*), "You shall have no other gods before Me."

Such a person is counted as one who denies the fundamental principle (*Kofer BeIkkar*), since this is the great principle upon which everything else depends.

1:7 God is one. He is not two nor more than two, but One.

His unity, however, is like none other in the world.

He is not one like a species, which still encompasses many individuals.

He is not one like a physical thing, which can be divided into parts and dimensions.

19

He is one with a Unity that is absolutely unique.

If there were many deities, then they would have to have bodies and physical existence. This is because similar things can only be separated through their physical qualities.

If God were physical, then he would have to be finite. This is because it is impossible for anything physical to be infinite. If His body were finite, however, then His power would also be finite.[1]

But we know that God's power is infinite and continuous... It is therefore not associated with anything physical. Since He is not physical, however, there can be no physical qualities separating Him from another similar being.

There can therefore only be one God.

To know this is a commandment of the Torah. It is thus written (*Deuteronomy 6:4*), "Hear, O Israel, the Lord is our God, the Lord is One."

Code, Repentance
(Yad, Tshuvah)

3:7 Five are in the category of the nonbeliever (*Min*): ... One who admits that the world has a Master, but says that there are two or more.

Points for Discussion

1. What do we mean when we say that God's unity is unique?

2. Would you describe God as being simple? If so, can you imagine anything as simple as God?

3. Can God exist in space? Can the concept of position apply to Him?

4. The main difference between the physical and the spiritual involves the concept of space. If there is no space in the spiritual realm, then how are things differentiated? Explain the statement, "Equal things can only be separated by their physical qualities." Is position one of these qualities?

5. Can an absolute unity such as God exist in two different times? How then would the concept of time apply to Him? Explain the statement in the second principle, "He was, He is, and He will be." Why is this included in this principle?

6. Can an absolute unity be visible? What would you see? Discuss this in the context of *Yigdal*.

7. Can an absolute unity be bounded? By what would it be bounded? Again, discuss this in the context of *Yigdal*.

8. Discuss the Christian concept of the Trinity in the light of this principle.

בֶּאֱמוּנָה שְׁלֵמָה
שֶׁהַבּוֹרֵא, יִתְבָּרַךְ שְׁמוֹ,
אֵינוֹ גוּף,
וְלֹא יַשִׂיגוּהוּ
מַשִׂיגֵי הַגוּף,
וְאֵין לוֹ
שׁוּם דִּמְיוֹן כְּלָל.

The Third Principle

I believe with perfect faith that God does not have a body. Physical concepts do not apply to Him. There is nothing whatsoever that resembles Him at all.

Yigdal

He does not have bodily form, he is not a body,
He is beyond compare in His holiness.

Commentary on Mishnah

The third principle is that God is totally nonphysical.

We believe that this Unity [which we call God] is not a body or a physical force.

Nothing associated with the physical can apply to Him in any way.

We thus cannot say that God moves, rests, or exists in a given place. Things such as this can neither happen to Him, nor be part of His intrinsic nature.

When our sages speak of God, they therefore teach that such concepts as combination and separation do not apply to Him. They say in the Talmud (*Chagiga 15a*), "On high, there is neither sitting nor standing, neither combination nor separation."[2]

The Prophet says (*Isaiah 40:25*), "'To whom will you liken Me? To what am I equal?' says the Holy One." If God were physical then He would resemble other physical things.

In many places, however, our holy scriptures do speak of God in physical terms. Thus, we find such concepts as walking, standing, sitting and speaking used in relation to God. In all these cases, though, scripture is only speaking metaphorically. Our sages teach us scripture is only speaking metaphorically. Our sages teach us (*Berachos 31b*), "The Torah speaks in the language of man."

The Torah teaches us this third principle when it says (*Deuteronomy 4:15*), "You have not seen any image." We cannot conceive of God as

25

having any image or form. This is because He is not a physical being or force, as discussed earlier.

Code, Foundations of the Torah
(Yad, Yesodey HaTorah)

1:8 It is clearly expressed in both the Torah and in the Prophets that God has neither a body nor any other physical attributes.

It is thus written (*Joshua 2:11*), "The Lord your God is God in the heavens above and on the earth beneath."[3] A physical body, however, cannot be in two places at the same time.

The Torah likewise says (*Deuteronomy 4:15*), "You have not seen any image."

God furthermore told His prophet (*Isaiah 40:25*), "To whom will you liken Me? To what am I equal?" If God were a physical being, then He would resemble other physical things.

1:9 Once we know this to be true, we might find it difficult to understand many passages in the Torah. We thus find such expressions as (*Exodus 24:10*), "beneath His feet," and (*Ibid. 31:18*), "written with God's finger." In many places we likewise find expressions such as "the hand of God,"[4] "the eyes of God,"[5] and "the ears of God."[6]

All these expressions are actually adaptations to human intellect, which can only think in terms of the physical. The Torah thus speaks in the language of man.

They are all metaphors. For example, we find in the Torah such expressions as (*Deuteronomy 32:41*), "I will sharpen My flashing sword." Can we then say that God has a sword, or that He needs a sword with which to kill? We understand, however, that the expression is used allegorically. The same is true of all similar expressions.

We can substantiate this view from the fact that different prophets describe God in utterly different ways. Thus, one prophet says that he perceived God (*Daniel 7:9*), "with a garment as white as snow." Another prophet describes Him (*Isaiah 63:1*), "with His garments stained red." Moses himself saw God at the Red Sea like a mighty man waging war, while at Sinai, he visualized Him as a prayer leader, wrapped [in his Tallis].[7]

From all this, we see that God has no form or figure. What is seen is merely a prophetic visualization.

God's true nature is beyond the reach of human intellect. Man is simply incapable of grasping or understanding God. We thus find (*Job 11:7*), "Can you by searching fathom God? Can you fathom the Almighty to perfection?"

1:10 We must then understand what Moses meant when he asked of God (*Exodus 33:18*), "Show me Your glory."[8]

What Moses desired was to know the true nature of God. He wanted to comprehend this as well as one knows a person when he sees his face. In such a case, the person's features are engraved in one's mind, and he is seen as an individual, distinct from all others.

This is what Moses desired. He wanted to comprehend God's nature to such a degree that it would be separated in his mind from everything else in existence.

God replied to Moses that this was impossible. The intellect of a living man, consisting of body and soul, could not possibly comprehend this. [He thus told Moses (*Ibid. 33:20*), "You cannot see My face, for no man can see Me and live."]

But God did reveal things to Moses that had never before been revealed, and which never again will be revealed. In his mind, Moses was thus able to distinguish God from everything else that exists. But it was only like seeing a person's back, where all that can be seen is his body and clothing. One can still distinguish him as an individual [but it is not the same as when one sees his face]. The Torah alludes to this when it says [that God told Moses] (*Ibid. 33:23*), "You will see My back, but My face shall not be seen."

1:11 Since God is not a body or any other kind of physical entity, it is obvious that nothing associated with the physical can apply to Him.

We cannot apply to Him such concepts as combination and separation, position and size, up and down, right and left, back and front, sitting and standing.

He likewise does not exist in time. Such concepts as beginning, end and age therefore do not apply to Him.

God furthermore does not change, since there is nothing that can cause Him to change.

We therefore cannot apply to Him such concepts as life and death in a physical sense. We cannot use such terms as wisdom and foolishness in the same sense as we do when speaking of a human being. Such states as sleep and wakefulness, anger and laughter, joy and sadness, do not apply to Him at all. He does not keep quiet, nor does He speak as a person does.

Our sages thus teach us, "On high there is neither sitting not standing, neither combination nor separation."

1:12 We must therefore realize that whenever the Torah or Prophets speak about God, they do so in a metaphorical and allegorical manner.

This is true of the expressions mentioned earlier. It is also true of such expressions as (*Psalm 2:4*), "He who sits in the heavens shall laugh," (*Deuteronomy 32:21*), "They have provoked Me to anger with their vanity," and (*Ibid. 28:63*), "As God rejoices..." Regarding all such statements, our sages say that "the Torah speaks in the language of man." God Himself told His prophet (*Jeremiah 7:19*), "Do they indeed provoke Me to anger?"

God told the prophet (*Malachi 3:6*), "I am God, I do not change." But if God would be happy at some times and angry at others, he would indeed change. [It is therefore obvious that none of these states can apply to Him at all.]

All these states only exist in physical beings, living in this lowly dark world. We "dwell in houses of clay, whose foundation is in the dust."[9] God, however, is above all these things.

Code, Repentance
(*Yad, Tshuvah*)
3:7   Five are in the category of the nonbeliever (*Min*): ... One who admits that there is one Master, but claims that He is physical or has a form.

Points for Discussion

1. How are the second and third principles related?

2. What does the Torah mean when it says that man was created in the "image of God?"

3. Why does the Torah speak of God as if He were just like us?

4. Could Christianity accept this principle?

5. What nonphysical things affect our lives? Do these in any way resemble God?

6. Why is it impossible to comprehend God?

7. Why must the Torah speak in the language of man?

8. What do we mean when we say that God is holy? Relate this to the verse in *Yigdal*.

9. Why do we refer to God as "He," using the masculine gender?

אֲנִי מַאֲמִין

בֶּאֱמוּנָה שְׁלֵמָה
שֶׁהַבּוֹרֵא, יִתְבָּרַךְ שְׁמוֹ,
הוּא רִאשׁוֹן
וְהוּא אַחֲרוֹן.

The Fourth Principle

I believe with perfect faith that God is first and last.

Yigdal
He preceded all things that were created,
He is first, yet without beginning.

Commentary on Mishnah
The fourth principle involves the absolute eternity of the One [whom we call God]. Nothing else shares His eternal quality. This is discussed many times in Scripture, and the Torah teaches it to us when it says of Him (*Deuteronomy 33.27*), "The eternal God is a refuge."

Code, Repentance
(*Yad, Tshuva*)
3:8 Five are in the category of the nonbeliever (*Min*): ... One who says that God alone was not the first thing and Creator of all.

Guide to the Perplexed
(*Moreh Nevuchim*)
2:13 Everything (other than God Himself) was created by God out of absolute nothingness. In the beginning, God alone existed. There was nothing else... He then created everything that exists from absolute nothingness. It all followed His will and desire.

Even time itself is among the things created by God. Time depends upon motion. In order for motion to exist, we must have things that move. And all things were created by God.

Points for Discussion

1. How is this principle related to the previous one?

2. Discuss the following questions: What existed before the first thing? Who created the first thing?

3. Children often ask, "Who created God?" Discuss this question.

4. What do we mean when we say that God is last?

5. Why do we consider time as something that was created?

אֲנִי מַאֲמִין

בֶּאֱמוּנָה שְׁלֵמָה
שֶׁהַבּוֹרֵא, יִתְבָּרַךְ שְׁמוֹ,
לוֹ לְבַדּוֹ
רָאוּי לְהִתְפַּלֵּל,
וְאֵין רָאוּי לְהִתְפַּלֵּל
לְזוּלָתוֹ.

The Fifth Principle

I believe with perfect faith that it is only proper to pray to God. One may not pray to anyone or anything else.

Yigdal
He is the Lord of the world, and all things created,
Display His greatness and His majesty.

Commentary on Mishnah
The fifth principle teaches us that God is the only one whom we may serve and praise. We may sing only of His greatness and obey only His commandments.

We may not act in this way toward anything beneath Him, whether it be an angel, a star, one of the elements, or any combination of them. All these have a predetermined nature and, therefore, none can have authority or free will. Only God has these attributes.

It is therefore not proper to serve these things or make them intermediaries to bring us closer to God. All our thoughts should be directed only toward Him. Nothing else should even be considered.

This fifth principle forbids all forms of idolatry, and it constitutes a major portion of the Torah.

Code, Idolatry
(Yad, Avodas Kochavim)
1:1 In the days of Enosh, mankind succumbed to a grave error, demolishing the advice of the wise men living in that time. Enosh himself was among those who were caught up in this mistaken idea.[10]

This was their error:

They argued that God created stars and spheres with which to control the world, placing them on high and giving them honor. These creations are then the servants who minister to Him and it is therefore fitting to praise, glorify and honor them. Certainly God would want us to honor and praise those whom He Himself elevates and honors. They compared God to an earthly king, who wishes his subjects to honor those who stand before him, since this in itself demonstrates their respect for the king.

Following this false line of reasoning, they began to build temples to the stars and offer them sacrifices. They praised and glorified them with words, and bowed down before them. They [Enosh and his contemporaries] had become so confused and mistaken that they felt they were actually fulfilling God's will in this manner.

This is the foundation of idol worship.

Idolators who really understand their belief also conceive it in this way. They never claim that there is no God other than the star that they worship.

The Prophet Jeremiah spoke of this when he said (*Jeremiah 10:7, 9*), "Who would not fear You, O King of nations? It is Your due. For among all the wise ones of the nations and their kingdoms, there is none like You. For in one respect they are fools and simpletons: the vanities that they preach are nothing more than a block of wood."[11] They all know that God is unique. But their error is in thinking that their [idolatry, which is really] foolishness is God's will.

2:1   The main commandment regarding idolatry is not to worship anything that God created, whether it be an angel, a sphere, a star, one of the elements, or anything created from them.

Even though one knows that God is the true God, and only worships this thing in the manner that Enosh and his generation first did, he is still an idolator.

The Torah thus warns us (*Deuteronomy 4:19*), "Do not lift your eyes to the heavens, and see the sun, [moon and stars, and all the host of heaven, and be drawn to worship and serve them] which the Lord your God has allotted to all peoples." You shall not let your mind's eye rove and think that these control the world. You might see that they continue to exist and do not deteriorate, and then mistakenly think that one must bow down to them and serve them.

The Torah likewise says (*Deuteronomy 11:16*), "Watch yourselves, lest your hearts be deceived [and you turn aside and serve other gods and worship them]." You should not be deceived by the thoughts of your hearts to serve these and make them intermediaries between you and God.

Code, Repentance
(Yad, Tshuvah)

3:7 Five are in the category of the nonbeliever (*Min*): ... One who serves a star or constellation in order that it be an advocate between him and the Master of all worlds.

Points for Discussion

1. Why is idolatry forbidden?

2. Why is it forbidden to worship an angel if one still believes in God? Why is this an error?

3. Christianity teaches that one can only approach God through Jesus. How would this principle apply to that belief?

4. How does belief in idolatry diminish our concept of God?

5. How does the verse in *Yigdal* relate to this principle?

6. An earthly king depends upon his subordinates to help him rule. Is this true of God? How does this relate to this principle?

אֲנִי מַאֲמִין

בֶּאֱמוּנָה שְׁלֵמָה
שֶׁכָּל־דִּבְרֵי נְבִיאִים
אֱמֶת.

The Sixth Principle

I believe with perfect faith that all the words of the prophets are true.

Yigdal
He has granted the bounty of His prophecy
To the men of His choice and glory.

Commentary on Mishnah
The sixth principle concerns prophecy.

We must realize that there exist human beings who have such lofty qualities and achieve such great perfection that their souls become prepared to receive pure spiritual wisdom.

Their human intellect can then become bound up with the Creative Mind (*Sechel HaPo'el*), and receive an inspired emanation from it. This is prophecy, and those people who achieve it are the prophets.

This is the concept of prophecy. A full explanation would require a lengthy discussion, but we do not intend here to cite proof-texts for every principle or explain how prophecy is attained. In passing, however, I will remind you that many verses in the Torah testify to the prophecy of many different prophets.

Code, Foundations of the Torah
(Yad, Yesodey HaTorah)
7:1 It is a foundation of our faith to know that God grants prophecy to man.

Such prophecy can only be attained by a person who has very great intelligence. He must have strong character, and not be overcome by his impulses in any way. He must also have constant control over his emotions and have an outlook that is both very broad and very firm.[12]

A person having all these qualities can then delve into the spiritual.[13] He can advance in these deep, subtle concepts, gaining a firm understanding and perception of them.

At the same time, he must also sanctify himself and separate himself from the ways of the common people, who grope in the darkness of the times. He must achieve a constant diligence in not even thinking of non-essentials or considering the vanities and intrigues of the times.

He must work upon himself until his mind is constantly clear and directed on high. He must bind his intellect to the Throne of Glory, striving to comprehend the purity and holiness of the spiritual beings. He must furthermore contemplate the wisdom of God in everything and understand its significance, whether it be the highest spiritual entity or the lowliest thing on earth.

One who does this immediately becomes worthy of Divine Inspiration (*Ruach HaKodesh*).[14]

When one attains this spirit [of inspiration], his soul becomes bound up in the level of the angels...and he becomes a different individual completely. He can now understand things with a knowledge completely different than anything he ever had previously. The level that he has attained is far above that of other men who can merely use their intellect.

This is the meaning of what [the prophet Samuel told] King Saul (*1 Samuel 10:6*): "[The spirit of God will descend upon you,] and you shall prophesy with them, and you shall be transformed into a different man."

7:2 There are many levels of prophecy. Just as one person may have greater intelligence than another, so one prophet can be greater in prophecy than another.

All prophets, however, have one thing in common. They all see their prophecy only in a dream or vision at night, or else during the day while in a trance. This is what the Torah means when it says (*Numbers 12:6*), "[If there be a prophet among you, then I, God,] will make Myself known to him in a vision—I will speak to him in a dream."

Prophecy is also a very traumatic experience. The prophet's limbs tremble, his body becomes faint, and he loses control of his thoughts. All that remains in his consciousness is a clear understanding of what he is experiencing.

We thus find in the case of Abraham (*Genesis 15:12*), "[Abraham fell into a trance,] and a great dark dread fell upon him." Similarly, Daniel describes his vision, saying (*Daniel 10:8*), "[I saw this great vision, and I became powerless.] My appearance was destroyed, and my strength deserted me. [I heard the sound of his words, and I fell on the ground in a trance.]"

7:3 When a prophet is given a message, it is given in the form of an allegory. The interpretation of the allegory, however, is immediately implanted in his mind, and he knows its meaning.

Thus, for example, Jacob saw a ladder with angels going up and down on it. This was an allegory for the empires that would subjugate his children.[15]

The same was true of other prophets. Ezekiel saw a vision of living creatures.[16] Jeremiah saw a boiling pot[17] and an almond tree rod.[18] Ezekiel also saw a scroll,[19] and Zechariah, a measure.[20]

In these instances, the Prophet divulged both the allegory and its interpretation. In some cases, only the interpretation was revealed. Other times, only the allegory was recorded, and this is true of some of the prophecies of Ezekiel and Zechariah. All the prophets, however, only prophesized by means of allegories and methaphors.[21]

7:4 A prophet cannot prophesy at will. He must concentrate and seclude himself in a good, joyous mood. For one cannot attain prophecy when he is depressed or languid, but only when he is joyous.[22]

The prophets would therefore have people play music for them when they were seeking prophecy.[23] We find (*1 Samuel 10:5*), "[A band of prophets, coming from a high place, led by harp, drum, flute and lyre,] and they were seeking prophecy." That is, they were seeking to be worthy of a prophetic vision.

7:5 Those seeking prophecy were known as the "sons of the prophets."[24] Even though they did everything properly, it was possible that the Divine Presence would descend upon them, but it was also possible that it would not.

7:7 Sometimes a prophet experiences prophecy only for his sake alone. It then comes to broaden his outlook, increase his knowledge, and help him to learn more about these lofty concepts.

At other times, a prophet may be sent to a group of people, a city, or a national government. He then comes to prepare and instruct them, or to keep them from evil that they are doing.

When such a prophet is sent, he is given a sign or miracle in order to show the people that he was actually sent by God.

However, we do not accept everyone who performs a sign or miracle as a prophet. First, he must demonstrate that he is fit for prophecy. He must be outstanding in his generation, both in wisdom and in piety, and must follow the holy paths of prophecy, separating himself from all worldly things. Only then do we accept him when he performs a sign or miracle and says that God sent him.

When this happens we are commanded to obey such a prophet. The Torah thus says (*Deuteronomy 18:15*), "[God will raise up a prophet from among you...] and you shall harken to him."

It is, of course, always possible that one may perform a sign or miracle and still not be a prophet. The miracle can always have something else behind it. Still, we are commanded to obey such a prophet. We see that he is a great sage, fit for prophecy, and we therefore accept him as such.

We find a very similar case in the Torah. We are commanded to judge all legal cases on the basis of the testimony of two witnesses.[25] It is always possible that these witnesses may be lying, but we must still accept them, since they fulfill all our requirements.

The Torah therefore says (*Deuteronomy 29:28*), "Secret things are for the Lord our God, but what we can see is for us and for our children." It is likewise written (*I Samuel 16:7*), "Man sees with his eyes, but [only] God sees into the heart."

10:1 When a prophet comes and claims to be sent by God, it is not necessary that he perform miracles like those of Moses, Elijah and Elisha, which actually violated the laws of nature. All that he must do is accurately predict the future. The Torah thus says (*Deuteronomy 18:21, 22*), "If you say in your heart, 'How can we know that the word [was not spoken by God?' If the prophet speaks in God's name, and the word does not come true, then that word was not spoken by God, and the prophet has spoken deceitfully." From this, we also see the converse.]

All that is therefore required is that the individual be fit for prophecy in his relationship to God. He must furthermore not teach that we add to or subtract from [the Torah], but only that we serve God according to its commandments. We merely say, "If you are a true prophet, then predict the future." He must then do so, and we wait to see whether or not his prediction comes true.

If even a single detail of his prediction does not come true, then we can be certain that this individual is a false prophet. If his prediction is completely accurate, we accept him.

10:2 We must then test this prophet a number of times. If his predictions all come true, then he is a true prophet. We thus find in the case of Samuel (*Samuel 3:18, 19*), "[Samuel grew, and God was with him, and not one of his words did not come true.] And all Israel, from Dan to Beersheba, knew that Samuel had become established as a prophet of God."

10:3 We might find that horoscopists and fortunetellers also predict the future, but there is a vast difference between them and a true prophet. Even though a fortuneteller might predict the future, he cannot do so with unerring accuracy. Some predictions may come true, but many others do not. We thus find (*Isaiah 47:13*), "Let now the astrologers, stargazers and fortunetellers stand up, and tell you *something* of what will come upon you." They can only tell you *something*, but not everything.

It is also possible that none of their predictions will come true at all. It thus written (*Isaiah 44:25*), "He frustrates the signs of imposters, and makes fortunetellers look foolish."

The predictions of a [true] prophet, however, must all come true. We find (*I Kings 10:10*), "No word of God shall fall to the ground." God likewise told His prophet (*Jeremiah 23:28*), "Let the prophet who has a dream tell that dream, and let he who has My word speak the truth, for how does straw compare to wheat?" The predictions of fortunetellers and mediums are like straw, which may have a little wheat mixed with it. But God's word is like pure wheat, containing no straw at all.

The Torah teaches us that even when these astrologers and fortunetellers do predict the future, they are still charlatans. We learn truth from the prophets, and have no need for such things as mediums and horoscopists. The Torah tells us (*Deuteronomy 18:10-15*), "There shall not be anyone among you [...who uses divination, fortunetelling, augury or divination...] For the other nations [...harken to fortunetellers. But God does not permit you to do such things.] God will raise up a prophet from among you..."

We see from this that one of the main tasks of the prophet is to tell us the future and predict such things as bounty and famine, war and peace. Even the needs of an individual may be revealed to a prophet. Thus, when Saul lost something, he went to a prophet, who then told him where it was.[27]

This is the main task of the prophet. He does not come to start a new religion, or to add to or subtract from the commandments of the Torah.

10:4 A prophet may sometimes predict troubles, saying that an individual will die, that a famine will occur, or the like. In such cases, the fact that his predictions do not come true does not invalidate his status as a prophet.[28]

In such cases, we do not say that he failed in his prediction. We know that God is "slow to anger, rich in kindness and regretting evil."[29] It is therefore always possible that the people have repented and been forgiven by God. This indeed happened in such cases as when [Jonah warned]

Nineveh.[30] It is also possible that God may have suspended their judgement, as in the case of Hezekiah.[31]

If a prophet predicts good, however, and it does not come true, then we can be certain he is a false prophet. Anything good that God decrees is not retracted, even if it is only stated conditionally.[32]

There was actually only one case where God reversed a good prediction. Before the destruction of the First Temple (*Bais HaMikdash*), God promised that the righteous would not be killed together with the wicked. In this one case, God retracted His word [and the righteous were also destroyed]. This is explained in detail [in the Talmud] in the tract of *Shabbos*.[33]

A prophet is therefore only tested through a good prediction. We see this in Jeremiah's answer to Hananiah son of Azzur. Jeremiah was prophesying that evil would come, while Hananiah was predicting good. Jeremiah then told Hananiah, "If my prediction does not come true, it does not prove me to be a false prophet [since I am predicting evil]. But if yours does not come true, it shall be known that you are false [since you are predicting good]." We also find (*Jeremiah 28:7,9*), "Now listen to this... When a prophet predicts peace, and his words come true, then it shall be known that he is the prophet who is truly sent by God."[34]

10:5   If an established prophet testifies that another is a true prophet, we accept the latter without any further test. Thus, we see that after Moses testified regarding him, Joshua was accepted by all Israel, even before he provided any sign.[35] The same was true for all future generations.

Once a prophet is established and his predictions come true time after time, it is forbidden to suspect him or think that his prophecy is not true. As long as he follows the ways of prophecy, it is forbidden to test him unduly.

We therefore do not continually test a prophet. The Torah says (*Deuteronomy 6:16*), "You shall not test the Lord your God as you did at Massah." [It was at Massah that the people doubted the prophecy of Moses and asked for a further test,] saying (*Exodus 17:7*), "Is God among us or not?"

Once it is determined that an individual is a prophet, we must know and believe that God is among us and not disparage this prophet. We thus find [that God told Ezekiel], (*Ezekiel 33:33*), "[When it comes true—and it *will* come true—] then they will know that a prophet has been among them."[36]

Code, Repentance
(Yad, Tshuvah)

Three are in the category of the heretic (*Apikores*): One who says that prophecy does not exist, and that there is no way in which God communicates information to man.

Points for Discussion

1. How do we know what is good and what is evil? How are these things defined?

2. What do we mean when we say that Judaism is a revealed religion?

3. How does a revealed religion differ from other philosophies? What makes it superior?

4. Why is prophecy one of the fundamental principles of Judaism?

5. What is a prophet? How does one become a prophet?

6. Do prophets exist today? Why?

7. What conditions must be fulfilled before we accept someone as a prophet?

8. What is the relationship between music and prophecy? How does this relate to your own experience?

9. Why is predicting the future a hallmark of prophecy?

10. What does this principle teach us about the Bible?

בֶּאֱמוּנָה שְׁלֵמָה
שֶׁנְּבוּאַת מֹשֶׁה רַבֵּנוּ,
עָלָיו הַשָׁלוֹם,
הָיְתָה אֲמִתִּית,
וְשֶׁהוּא הָיָה
אָב לַנְּבִיאִים,
לַקּוֹדְמִים לְפָנָיו
וְלַבָּאִים אַחֲרָיו.

The Seventh Principle

I believe with perfect faith that the prophecy of Moses is absolutely true. He was the chief of all prophets, both before and after him.

Yigdal

There has not arisen another like Moses,
A prophet who looked upon His image.

Commentary on Mishnah

The seventh principle involves Moses.

We believe that Moses was the chief of all prophets.[37] He was superior to all other prophets, whether they preceded him or arose afterwards.

Moses attained the highest possible human level. He perceived the Godly to a degree surpassing every human being that ever existed. He literally elevated himself from the level of the mere human to that of an angel.

Moses himself thus became like an angel. There was no barrier that he did not split and penetrate. Nothing physical held him back. He was not tainted by any deficiency, great or small. His thoughts, senses and feelings ceased to exist entirely. His conscious mind was completely separated and became a pure spiritual being. It is for this reason that we say that he spoke to God without needing an angel as a mediator.

I would very much like to explain this mystery and unlock its secrets in the Torah. [In the Torah, God says of Moses] (*Numbers 12:8*), "Mouth to mouth, I will speak to him," and this entire passage requires considerable explanation.

Before I could delve into this, however, I would first have to cite many proofs, propositions, introductions, and examples. First, I would have to explain the nature of angels, and how they differ from God Himself. The soul and all its powers would also have to be explained. The discussion would then have to be expanded to include an exposition of all the images that the prophet used to describe God and the angels. This, in turn, would involve a discussion of the Divine Stature (*Shiur Komah*)[38] and all that it involves.

Even this would not suffice, and no matter how concise such a discussion would be, it would involve an essay of at least a hundred pages. I will therefore leave these matters for a book of discourses that I plan to write. Otherwise, I will include this discussion in a work on the prophets that I am currently writing, or in a special volume explaining these [thirteen] principles.

Returning to this seventh principle, let us distinguish Moses' prophecy from that of all other prophets in four ways:

1. God spoke to all other prophets through an intermediary. Moses alone did not need any intermediary. This is what the Torah means when it says [in God's name] (*Numbers 12:8*), "Mouth to mouth, I will speak to him."

2. Every other prophet could only receive prophecy while sleeping. We therefore find in numerous places that prophecy is described as (*Genesis 20:3*), "a dream at night," and (*Job 33:15*), "a vision of night." If prophecy does occur during the day, it only comes when the prophet falls into a trance, where all his senses are obliterated and his mind becomes as passive as in a dream. This state is called a "vision" or an "insight."[39] To Moses, however, the word came by day, when he stood [fully awake] before the two cherubim. God Himself thus testified (*Exodus 25:22*), "I will meet with you there [and I will speak with you, from above the ark-cover, from between the two cherubim that are on the ark of testimony]." God likewise said (*Numbers 12:6-8*), "If there be a prophet among you, [then I, God, will make Myself known to him in a vision, I will speak to him in a dream]. This is not true of My prophet Moses... Mouth to mouth, I will speak to him."

3. Even though other prophets only experienced a vision in a trance, and then, only through an angel, it was still a very traumatic experience for them. Their strength would fail, their stature would become disarrayed, and they would experience such dread that they would come close to death. After the angel Gabriel spoke to Daniel in a vision, Daniel said (*Daniel 10:8*), "I became powerless, my appearance was disarrayed, and my strength deserted me...and I fell on the ground in a trance." He later said (*Ibid. 10:16*), "The vision caused me to become dislocated [and I had no strength left]." This, however, was not true of Moses. The word came to him without his experiencing any trembling or terror whatsoever. The Torah thus says (*Exodus 33:11*), "God spoke to Moses face to face, as a man speaks to his friend." Moses' prophecy was just like a friendly conversation, involving no agitation whatsoever.

Moses did not tremble at the word, even though it was "face to face."
This was because he was so completely attached to the spiritual, as discussed earlier.

4. Other prophets could not receive prophecy whenever they desired.
It all depended on God's will. A prophet might wait days and years and
still not achieve prophecy. All that he could do was plead to God to reveal a vision and then wait until it came. This might take days and
months, and sometimes it might not ever come. There were numerous
groups who purified their minds and constantly kept themselves in preparation for prophecy. We are told that when he sought prophecy, Elisha
said (*2 Kings 3:15*), "Now bring me a musician." Still even with this preparation, it was not certain that he would attain prophecy. Moses, on the
other hand, could achieve prophecy whenever he desired. The Torah
quotes him as saying (*Numbers 9:8*), "Now wait, and I will hear what
God commands in your case." God likewise told Moses (*Leviticus 16:2*),
"Speak to Aaron your brother that he not come at all times into the
holy place." Our sages teach us that this means Aaron could not approach God whenever he pleased, but Moses could.[41]

Code, Foundations of the Torah
(Yad, Yesoday HaTorah)

7:6 Moses was the master of all other prophets. There are therefore
numerous differences between Moses and all others.

All other prophets could only achieve prophecy in a dream or vision,
while Moses could prophesy while standing fully awake. The Torah thus
says (*Numbers 7:89*), "When Moses came into the Tent of Meeting (*Ohel
Moed*) to speak to God, he heard the Voice speaking to him."

All other prophets only received prophecy through an angel.[42] All that
they could see was an allegory or metaphor. Moses, however, did not receive his prophecy through any angel. God tells us (*Numbers 12:8*),
"Mouth to mouth, I will speak to him." In another place the Torah says
(*Exodus 33:11*), "God spoke to Moses face to face." We also find
(*Numbers 12:8*), "He (Moses) gazes upon a vision of God." This teach
us that Moses did not see a mere allegory. He saw the thing as it was,
without having to resort to any metaphor. The Torah thus says (*Ibid.*),
"[I speak to him...] manifestly, and not in allegory." Moses did not see
an allegorical vision, but was able to see things as they truly are.

All other prophets were terrorized, confused and torn apart by their
experience. This was not true of Moses, as the Torah says (*Exodus 33:11*),
"[God spoke to Moses...] as a man speaks to his friend." A man is not

terrorized by his friend's conversation. Moses likewise had enough mental strength to understand words of prophecy with his composure totally unaffected. All other prophets could not achieve prophecy whenever they desired. This was not true of Moses. Whenever he wished, he could be enveloped by Divine Inspiration (*Ruach HaKodesh*), and prophecy would descend upon him. He would not have to concentrate and prepare himself for it, for he was in a constant state of concentration and preparation, just like a ministering angel. He could therefore prophesy at all times, and the Torah quotes him as saying (*Numbers 9:8*), "Now wait, and I will hear what God commands in your case."

God promised this to Moses when he said (*Deuteronomy 5:27,28*), "Go say to them, 'Return now to your tents.' But you stand here with Me [and I will speak to you]." We see from this that all other prophets had to return "to their tents"—to their worldly needs—after they were finished with their prophecy. They were once again like all other people, and therefore did not have to separate from their wives. Moses, on the other hand, never returned to his "first tent," and never again touched a woman.[43] His mind was continually bound to the Creator of all worlds, and the glory never left him. He became as holy as an angel. The Torah thus says that (*Exodus 34:29*), "the skin of his face sent forth beams of light."

8:1 The Jewish people did not believe in Moses because of any miracles that he might have performed. For when one believes in something because of miracles, he still may have doubts and suspect that they might have been performed by means of magic or trickery. All the miracles that Moses performed in the desert, however, were only done because they were necessary, and not to bring proof of his prophecy.

Thus, when it was necessary to defeat the Egyptians, he split the sea and saved us in its midst.[44] When we needed food, he provided us with the Manna.[45] When we were thirsty, he split the rock [to provide water].[46] When Korach and his band revolted, he caused the earth to swallow them up.[47] The same is true of all his other miracles.

But the main reason why we believe in Moses, is because of what happened at Mount Sinai. "Our eyes saw, and not a stranger's."[48] Our ears heard, and not another's. There was the fire, the thunder and lightning,[49] when Moses entered in the deep clouds.[50] The Voice spoke to him, and we ourselves heard it say, "Moses, Moses, speak to the people." Moses thus told the people (*Deuteronomy 5:4*), "Face to face, God spoke to you." The Torah likewise says (*Ibid. 5:3*), "God did not make this covenant with our fathers [but with us, who are all here alive today]."

The revelation at Sinai is the only real proof that Moses' prophecy was true and contained no trickery. God told Moses (*Exodus 19:9*), "Behold, I come to you in a thick cloud, so that the people may hear when I speak with you, so that they may believe in you forever." Before Sinai, the people did not believe with a faith strong enough to last forever. They might have believed, but they could have later had doubts and suspicions.

Those who received Moses' message were therefore themselves witnesses that his prophecy was true, and no further sign was needed.

Moses and the Jewish people were like two witnesses who have seen the same thing. Each witness in the pair knows that the other is speaking truthfully, and neither one needs any proof regarding the other. The same is true of Moses. The entire Jewish people were his witnesses after the revelation at Sinai, and no further signs were needed.

At the beginning of Moses' career, he was given miracles to perform in Egypt, and God told him (*Exodus 3:18*), "They shall harken to your voice." But Moses knew that one who only believes because of miracles still has doubts, suspicions and similar thoughts. He therefore did not want to go, and told God (*Ibid. 4:1*), "They will not believe me." God then told him that the miracles were only to establish the faith until after the Exodus. After that, they would stand at Mount Sinai, and all suspicions would be removed. They would then know for certain that it was God who gave him the initial signs and sent him from the beginning, and they would no longer have any doubts. God therefore told Moses (*Ibid. 3:12*), "This shall be your [true] sign that I have sent you. When you bring the people out of Egypt, you shall serve God on this mountain."

Therefore, when any other prophet comes, we do not believe him merely because he performs miracles. Just because he produces a miracle, it does not mean that we must accept everything he says. The only reason we accept a prophet is because the Torah says that if he produces a sign (*Deuteronomy 18:15*), "you shall harken unto him."

This again is similar to the laws regarding evidence. Testimony offered by two witnesses is accepted as legal evidence, even though we can never know for certain that they are telling the truth. In the same way, we are commanded to harken to such a prophet, even though we do not know for certain that his sign is true and not a result of magic and trickery.

8:3   Therefore, if a prophet comes and attempts to refute Moses' prophecy, we do not accept him, no matter what great miracles he performs.[52] Moses' prophecy did not depend on any miracles, and therefore cannot be disputed by miracles. We saw and heard with our own eyes and ears, exactly as Moses himself did.

Here again we can use the example of witnesses. If witnesses testify to something, and a person has seen with his own eyes that it is not true, then he is not bound to accept their testimony. He knows for certain that they are false witnesses.

The Torah therefore says (*Deuteronomy 13:3, 4*), "[Even] if the sign or wonder comes to pass...you shall not harken to the words of that [false] prophet." He might produce signs and miracles, but he is coming to contradict what we have seen with our own eyes. We only believe the evidence of miracles because of a commandment given to us by Moses. We therefore cannot possible accept any sign that comes to contradict Moses. We ourselves heard and saw his revelation.

Code, Repentance
(Yad, Tshuvah)

Three are in the category of the heretic (*Apikores*):... One who denies the prophecy of Moses...

Points for Discussion

1. Why is Moses so central to Judaism?

2. Why is it so important that he be the greatest of all prophets?

3. We speak here about the prophecy of Moses. Exactly what is this prophecy?

4. What is the most important single book in Judaism?

5. Compare the verse in *Yigdal* with *Deuteronomy 34:10* and *Numbers 12:8*.

6. How would this principle apply to Christianity and Islam?

7. To what extent do miracles verify a prophet's authenticity?

8. How did Moses differ from all other prophets?

9. Will the Messiah be greater than Moses?

10. Why did Moses have to reach such a high degree of prophecy?

11. What sort of person was Moses?

אֲנִי מַאֲמִין

בֶּאֱמוּנָה שְׁלֵמָה
שֶׁכָּל־הַתּוֹרָה
הַמְצוּיָה עַתָּה בְּיָדֵינוּ,
הִיא הַנְּתוּנָה
לְמֹשֶׁה רַבֵּנוּ,
עָלָיו הַשָּׁלוֹם.

The Eighth Principle

I believe with perfect faith that the entire Torah that we now have is that which was given to Moses.

Yigdal
God gave a true Torah to His people,
Through His prophet, trusted in all His house.

Commentary on Mishnah
The eighth principle is that the Torah given to us by Moses originated from God. It is therefore called "God's word."

We do not know exactly how the Torah was transmitted to Moses. But when it was transmitted, Moses merely wrote it down like a secretary taking dictation. In this way, he wrote the events of his time and the other stories in the Torah, as well as the commandments.[54] Moses was therefore called a "secretary."

Every verse in the Torah is equally holy. The Torah might contain verses such as (*Genesis 10:6*), "the sons of Ham were Cush and Mizraim," (*Ibid. 36:39*), "his wife's name was Mehitabel," and (*Ibid. 36:12*), "Timneh was his concubine,"[55] alongside of (*Exodus 20:2*), "I am the Lord your God..." and (*Deuteronomy 6:4*), "Hear O Israel, [the Lord is our God, the Lord is One]." All these verses are perfectly equal. They all originate from God, and are all part of God's Torah, which is perfect, pure, holy, and true.[56]

The person who says that some passages were written by Moses of his own accord is considered by our prophets and sages to be the worst sort of nonbeliever, and a perverter of the Torah.[57] Such a person claims that the Torah must be divided into a core and a shell, and that the stories and history contained in it were written by Moses and are of no true benefit.

Such a person is in the category of those who say, "the Torah is not from heaven."[58] Our sages teach that this category includes even one who says the entire Torah was given by God with the exception of a single word, which was composed by Moses and not spoken by God.[59] Regarding such a person, the Torah says (*Numbers 15:31*), "He has despised the word of God [...his soul shall be utterly cut off]."

If one really understands the Torah, then he finds every word filled with wondrous wisdom. It contains a depth that can never be plumbed completely—"it is broader than the earth and wider than the sea."[60] One need only follow the example of King David, the annointed of God and Jacob, who prayed (*Psalm 119:18*), "Uncover my eyes, that I may behold the wonders of Your Torah."

The same is true of the accepted explanation of the Torah, which was also given by God. [Following this oral tradition,] we make such things as the Succah, Lulav, Shofar, Tzitzis and Tefillin in exactly the manner that God dictated to Moses. Moses transmitted this to us as a trustworthy messenger.

The Torah teaches us this principle when it says (*Numbers 16:28*), "Moses said, 'Through this you shall know that God sent me to do all these things, and I did not do it on my own accord."

Introduction to Yad

Every commandment given to Moses on Mount Sinai was given together with an explanation. God thus told Moses (*Exodus 24:12*), "[Come up to Me to the mountain...] and I will give you the tablets of stone, the Torah and instruction." "Torah" refers to the written Torah, while "instruction" is its interpretation. We are thus commanded to keep the Torah according to its interpretation. This interpretation is what we call the Oral Torah (*Torah SheBaal Peh*).[61]

Moses wrote the entire Torah with his own hand shortly before he passed away. He gave a copy to each tribe, and another Torah was placed in the Ark as a testimony.[62] [Moses thus told the Levites] (*Deuteronomy 31:26*), "Take this scroll of the Torah and place it [by the side of the ark of the covenant...]"

The interpretation, however, was not written down but was orally taught to the elders, Joshua, and the rest of the Jews. Moses therefore said (*Deuteronomy 13:1*), "All this word that I instruct you, you shall keep and obey." It is for this reason that it is called the Oral Torah.

Although the Oral Torah was not written down, it was taught by Moses to his council, which was made up of seventy elders.[63] Elazar, Pinchas and Joshua thus all received the tradition from Moses. Joshua, however, was Moses' main disciple, and he was given [responsibility for] the Oral Torah, and received special instruction in it.[64]

Joshua likewise taught this tradition orally as long as he lived. There were then many elders who received the tradition from Joshua...

Rabbi Judah, the son of Rabbi Simeon, was known as Our Holy Rabbi[65]...And it was Our Holy Rabbi who wrote the Mishnah.[66]

From the time of Moses until Our Holy Rabbi, there was no book from which the Oral Torah could be taught publicly. In each generation, however, a prophet or the head of the Sanhedrin would write down his own notes in order that he might remember what he learned from his teachers. He would then use these notes in his oral teachings. Everyone listening would also take notes according to his ability.[67]

Similar notes were taken on laws that were not transmitted from generation to generation, but were derived through the Thirteen Principles [which were used to expound the Torah][68] and agreed upon by the Sanhedrin.

This continued until the time of Our Holy Rabbi. He then gathered all the traditions, laws, explanations, and commentaries on the entire Torah, which had been handed down from Moses and expounded by the Sanhedrin in each generation. This was then all compiled into the book known as the Mishnah.[69]

The Mishnah was then publicly taught to the sages and revealed to all the Jews. Everyone wrote it down, and it was spread to every community. The Oral Torah was thus preserved and not forgotten.

The reason why Our Holy Rabbi broke the tradition [of leaving the Oral Torah unwritten] was because he saw that the number of students was declining, new troubles continually arising, and the Roman Empire spreading throughout the world and constantly becoming stronger. The Jews were also being separated, travelling to the four corners of the globe. He therefore wrote a single volume that everyone could have. It was something that could be learned rapidly and not forgotten.

Our Holy Rabbi spent all his life together with his council, publicly teaching the Mishnah.

Among the sages who were part of Our Holy Rabbi's council were...Rabbi Chiya, Rav, Bar Kapara...Rabbi Yochanan and Rabbi Hoshia... Besides these, there were tens of thousands of other sages who received the tradition [from Our Holy Rabbi].

Rav then wrote the *Sifra* and *Sifri* (commentaries on *Leviticus, Numbers* and *Deuteronomy*) to explain and expound upon the main points of the Mishnah. Rabbi Chiya wrote the *Tosefta* to elucidate other concepts in the Mishnah. Rabbi Hoshia and Bar Kapara likewise wrote *Beraisos* to explain the words of the Mishnah. Finally, Rabbi Yochanan wrote the Jerusalem Talmud, in the land of Israel, some 300 years after the destruction of the Holy Temple...

Ravina and Rav Ashi were the last of the sages of the Talmud. It was Rav Ashi who wrote the Babylonian Talmud in Babylon, approximately a hundred years after Rabbi Yochanan had written the Jerusalem Talmud.[70] Both Talmuds (or Gemorahs) were commentaries on the Mishnah, explaining its depth and expounding all the new concepts that had been resolved in the courts since the time of Our Holy Rabbi.

The two Talmuds, the *Tosefta*, the *Sifra* and the *Sifri* all explain what is permitted and forbidden, clean and unclean, liable and innocent, fit and unfit. It was all as it had been handed down from generation to generation, and ultimately from Moses himself...

Ravina and Rav Ashi were therefore the last great Jewish sages to transcribe the Oral Torah... Every Jew therefore follows the Babylonian Talmud... This is because every single Jew had agreed to accept the teachings of the Talmud...for it included the teachings of all our sages, or at least the majority of them. They, in turn had received the tradition regarding the foundations of the Torah from generation to generation, and ultimately from Moses himself...

Code, Repentance
(Yad, Tshuvah)

3:8 Three are in the category of those who deny the Torah: A person who says that the Torah does not come from God, even if he only says this with respect to one verse, or even one word. If a person says that Moses wrote it on his own, then he denies the Torah. The same is true of one who denies its interpretations as included in the Oral Torah. Such a person is then like Tzaduk and Baithus [who denied the Oral Torah].[71]

Code, Rebellion
(Yad, Mamrim)

1:1 [The Sanhedrin,] the great court in Jerusalem, is the basis of the Oral Torah. It stood as the pillar of Law, and from it laws and judgements emanated to all Israel. The Torah assures us [of this court's authority] when it says (*Deuteronomy 17:11*), "[You shall abide] by the Torah according to how they teach it to you." This in itself is a commandment of the Torah.

Everyone who believes in the Torah must therefore accept this court's authority and depend on it regarding all matters concerning our religion.

3:1 One who does not believe in the Oral Torah...is counted as a heretic (*Apikores*).

3:2 If one openly denies the authenticity of the Oral Torah, he is in the same category as all other heretics, people who deny that the Torah came from heaven, informers and renegades. All of these are not counted as Jews.

3:3 This is only true when one denies the Oral Torah on the basis of his own thoughts and opinions. This is the person who follows his own limited intellect and stubbornly denies the Oral Torah on his own. He thus follows the footsteps of Tzaduk, Baithus and their followers.

But this does not include the children of those who go astray or their descendants. These are raised among the Karaites[72] and are convinced by their parents. Such people are therefore in the same category as a person kidnapped by gentiles as an infant[73] and raised by them. He may not eagerly abide by the commandments, but he is like one under constraint.[74]

Even though such a child may later find out that he is a Jew and see Jews practicing their religion, he is still considered to be under constraint, since he was raised in such a misguided manner.

The same is true of those who follow the ways of their fathers who are Karaites who have strayed.

It is therefore fitting to bring them back and draw them with words of peace, until they return to the strength of the Torah.

Points for Discussion

1. How was the Book of Genesis written?

2. What was the role of Moses in writing the Torah?

3. Compare this principle with the previous one.

4. What part of the Torah is uniquely Jewish?

5. What is the Oral Torah? Where do we now find it?

6. Who were responsible for insuring that the Oral tradition remained accurate?

7. How was the Oral Torah put into writing? When?

8. Why was this not done until after the rise of Christianity?

9. How do we know how to read and translate the Torah? To what degree is this related to the oral tradition?

10. Where do we find the laws of Tefillin? Why?

11. Why was the Torah given in two parts, one written and the other oral?

12. Who were the Saducees, Tzadukim, Baithusians and Karaites? What happened to them? What groups correspond to them today?

13. What is the status of one who grows up without knowledge of Judaism? How is this related to the concept of the oral tradition?

אֲנִי מַאֲמִין

בֶּאֱמוּנָה שְׁלֵמָה
שֶׁזֹּאת הַתּוֹרָה
לֹא תְהִי מֻחְלֶפֶת,
וְלֹא תְהִי תּוֹרָה אַחֶרֶת
מֵאֵת הַבּוֹרֵא,
יִתְבָּרַךְ שְׁמוֹ.

The Ninth Principle

I believe with perfect faith that the Torah will not be changed, and that there will never be another Torah given by God.

Yigdal

God will not replace nor change His Law
For all time, for anything else.

Commentary on Mishnah

The ninth principle involves permanence. The Torah is God's permanent word, and no one else can change it.

Nothing can be added to or subtracted from either the written Torah or the Oral Torah. It is thus written (*Deuteronomy 13:1*), "You shall not add to it, nor subtract from it." This has already been discussed in detail in our introduction to this *Commentary on the Mishnah*.

Code, Foundations of the Torah
(Yad, Yesodey HaTorah)

9:1 The Torah clearly states that its commandments will remain binding forever, with neither change, addition nor subtraction. The Torah thus states (*Deuteronomy 13:1*), "All this word that I command you, you shall keep and do. You shall not add to it, not subtract from it." The Torah likewise says (*Ibid. 29:28*), "Things that are revealed belong to us and our children *forever*, to keep all the words of *this Torah*." We thus see that we are commanded to keep the words of the Torah forever. Similarly, with regard to many laws, the Torah clearly states, "It shall be an everlasting statute, for all your generations."[75]

The Torah furthermore says (*Ibid. 30:11, 12*), "[This commandment which I give you today...] is not in heaven." From this we learn that a prophet can no longer add anything to the Torah.[76]

Therefore, if any prophet comes to alter [the Torah, which is] the prophecy of Moses, we immediately know that he is a false prophet. It does not matter whether he is Jewish on non-Jewish, or how many signs or miracles he performs. If he says that God sent him to add or subtract a commandment of the Torah or explain it differently than our tradition from Moses, he is a false prophet. The same is true if he teaches that the commandments given to Israel were only given for a limited time and not forever...

In all such cases, we know that such a prophet is speaking presumptuously in God's name, making up something not told to him by God. For God Himself told Moses that this commandment (the Jewish religion) is "for us and for our children [forever]."

[And as the Torah says (*Numbers 23:19*),] "God is not man that He should speak falsely."

9:2   One may then wonder what God meant when He told Moses (*Deuteronomy 18:18*), "I will raise up a prophet like you from among your brothers."

But the truth is that such a prophet will not be sent to start any new religion. A prophet only comes to command us to keep the Torah and warn people who violate it. We thus find that the very last words of prophecy ever spoken were (*Malachi 3:22*), "Remember the Torah of Moses, My servant."

A prophet may likewise come to tell us things that have nothing at all to do with the commandments. Thus, for example, he might instruct us whether or not to go on a journey, wage a war, or build a wall. In such cases, we are commanded to obey his instructions...

Code, Repentance
(Yad, Tshuvah)

Three are in the category of those who deny the Torah:... One who says that God has exchanged His religion for another, or that the Torah no longer applies, even though it was originally from God.

Points for Discussion

1. Why do we believe that the Torah will never be changed or substituted?

2. Christianity claims that the Torah was the "old testament," which has now been replaced by a "new testament." How would this principle apply to their belief?

3. How does this principle apply to Islam?

4. Many Jews feel that the commandments of the Torah are no longer valid since "times have changed." Discuss this belief.

5. Does God know the future? When He gave the Torah, could He anticipate what the present world would be like?

6. The Torah contains commandments regarding many things, such as sacrifices and the laws of purity, which no longer apply. Why does this not contradict this principle?

7. Will we still keep the Torah in the Messianic Age?

8. Can anything in the Torah ever become "old fashioned?"

9. Did God give the world any religion other than Judaism?

בֶּאֱמוּנָה שְׁלֵמָה
שֶׁהַבּוֹרֵא, יִתְבָּרַךְ שְׁמוֹ,
יוֹדֵעַ כָּל־מַעֲשֵׂה
בְּנֵי אָדָם
וְכָל־מַחְשְׁבוֹתָם,
שֶׁנֶּאֱמַר:
הַיּוֹצֵר יַחַד לִבָּם,
הַמֵּבִין אֶל כָּל־מַעֲשֵׂיהֶם.

The Tenth Principle

I believe with perfect faith that God knows all of man's deeds and thoughts. It is thus written (Psalm 33:15), "He has molded every heart together, He understands what each one does."

Yigdal

He sees, He knows our secrets,
He sees each thing's end at its very beginning.

Commentary on Mishnah

The tenth principle is that God knows all that men do, and never turns His eyes away from them. It denies the opinion of those who say (*Ezekiel 9:9*), "God has abandoned His world. [God does not see.]"[77]

This principle is taught by the Prophet when he says that God is (*Jeremiah 32:19*), "great in counsel, mighty in insight, whose eyes are open to all the ways of man." We also find it assumed in the Torah in such places as (*Genesis 6:5*), "God saw that the evil of man on earth was very great," and (*Ibid. 18:20*), "The cry of Sodom and Gomorrah is great." These and similar passages all reflect this tenth principle.

Code, Foundations of the Torah
(Yad, Yesodey HaTorah)

2:9 Everything that exists (with the exception of God Himself) only exists because God gives it power to exist. This is true of everything, from the highest angelic form to the smallest insect in the interior of the earth.[78]

2:10 God knows Himself, and is aware of His own greatness, glory and reality, and He therefore must also know everything else. There is nothing that can be hidden from Him.[79]

God recognizes His true nature and knows it exactly as it is.

This knowledge is not something that can be separated from His essence. In this way, it is very different from ours. For our knowledge is not the same as our identity. But in the case of God, both He, His knowledge and His life are One. They are all One in every possible way and in the fullest definition of unity.

For if God lived with a "life" or knew with a "knowledge" that was not equivalent to His essence, then we would have to say that there was more than one God. For [neither His life nor His knowledge could be inferior to His essence, and therefore] we would have to say that there were many Gods. His essence, His life, and His knowledge [all being equal], would have to be considered [equally] as Gods.

This, of course, is not true. God is One in every possible way, in the fullest sense of unity.

We must therefore say that He Himself is the Knower, the thing that is known, and the knowledge itself.[80] It is all one.

This concept is beyond the power of speech to express, and beyond the power of the ear to hear. There is no way that the human mind can fully comprehend it.

We also know that this is true, however, from the very language of the scripture. When speaking of things other than God, it uses such expressions as "by the life of Pharaoh,"[81] and "by the life of your soul."[82] In the case of God, however, the scripture never uses the expression, "by the life *of* God." Rather, it always uses the expression, "by the Life— God."[83] This is because God and His life [are identical, and] not two separate entities, as in the case of physical beings and angels.

God therefore does not recognize and know creatures because of themselves, as we do. Rather, He knows them because of Himself. Everything depends upon Him for existence, and since He knows Himself, He therefore knows everything.

Code, Repentance
(Yad, Tshuvah)

5:5 We may then ask a very legitimate question. [For we find a paradox between God's knowledge of the future and man's freedom of will.] We must either say that God knows the future and therefore knows whether one will be good or wicked, or else we must say that He does not know. If we say that God knows a person will be good, then it is impossible for him to be otherwise. If, on the other hand, we say that God knows that he will be good, and it is still possible for him to be evil, then we must say that God's knowledge is not complete.[84]

Before going further, you must realize that the answer to this question is "wider than the earth, and broader than the sea."[85] It involves a great number of important basic principles and lofty concepts. However, you must pay very close attention to what I am saying.

In the second chapter of the Code, on the Foundations of the Torah (*Yesodey HaTorah*), we discussed the fact that God does not "know" with a knowledge that is separate from His essence. In the case of man, we can speak of the individual and his knowledge as two separate things. In the case of God, however, both He and His knowledge are one.

This, however, is beyond our power of understanding, just as man cannot understand God's true nature. This is what God meant [when He told Moses] (*Exodus 33:20*), "Man cannot see Me and live."

For the very same reason, man cannot understand God's knowledge. [God told us this through His] prophet, when He said (*Isaiah 55:8*), "My thoughts are not your thoughts, My ways are not your ways." We therefore do not have the ability to understand how God knows all things and deeds.

We know, however, without any doubt, that man has absolute free will, and that God does not force him nor decree upon him what to do. This is not only known from the traditions of our faith, but can also be proven philosophically. For this reason all prophecy teaches that man is judged for his deeds, and according to his deeds, whether they be good or evil. This is the foundation, and all prophecy depends upon it.

3:8 Three are in the category of the heretic (*Apikores*):... One who says that God does not know the deeds of man.

Points for Discussion

1. Why is this a fundamental principle? How is it related to the first principle?

2. If God does not change, how can He acquire knowledge?

3. Why do we say that God and His knowledge are one? Why are they not the same in the case of man?

4. Discuss the paradox of God's knowledge and free will. How does the Rambam treat this paradox?

5. Why is this paradox necessary? How can it strengthen our faith?

6. How does God know the future?

7. Why does the Rambam call free will the foundation of all prophecy?

8. How does God know our thoughts?

בֶּאֱמוּנָה שְׁלֵמָה
שֶׁהַבּוֹרֵא, יִתְבָּרַךְ שְׁמוֹ,
גּוֹמֵל טוֹב
לְשׁוֹמְרֵי מִצְוֹתָיו,
וּמַעֲנִישׁ לְעוֹבְרֵי מִצְוֹתָיו.

The Eleventh Principle

I believe with perfect faith that God rewards those who keep His commandments, and punishes those who transgress His commandments.

Yigdal

He rewards man with love, as his deeds deserve,
He gives the wicked evil, according to their wrong.

Commentary on Mishnah

The eleventh principle is that God rewards those who obey the commandments of the Torah, and punishes those who violate its prohibitions.

The greatest possible reward is the World to Come, while the greatest possible punishment is being cut of from it...

The Torah teaches us this principle in the following account. Moses said to God (*Exodus 32:32*), "If You will, then forgive their sin, but if not, then extinguish me." God answered (*Ibid. 32:33*), "The one who has sinned against Me, him will I erase from My book."

This shows that God knows both the obedient and the sinner, rewarding one and punishing the other.

Code, Repentance
(Yad, Tshuvah)

6:1 When either an individual or a nation sins...they deserve punishment, and God knows what punishment is fitting. In some cases one is punished through his body......, while in others he is punished through [the loss of] his possessions.

In other cases, his punishment might involve his minor children.[86] For young children, who are not yet obligated to keep the commandments, are considered like one's possessions.[87] The Torah says (*Deuteronomy 24:16*), "[Children shall not die because of their fathers,] every man shall die for his own sin." This, however, [does not refer to small children, but] only to an adult, who has full responsibility for his deeds.[88]

There are some cases in which a person is punished in the World to Come, and absolutely no harm comes to him in this world at all. In other cases, one may be punished both in this world and in the next.

6:2 This is only true when one does not repent. When a person repents, his repentance is like a shield protecting him from troubles.[89] And just as a person can sin through his own free will, so can he repent through his own free will.

8:1 The main reward of the righteous is in the World to Come. This is a life that is not terminated by death, and a good that is not mixed with any evil.

The Torah thus says (*Deuteronomy 22:7*), "You will have good, and your days will be long." Our traditions interpret this to say: "You will have a good"—in a world where all is good—"and your days will be long"—in a world that goes on and on.[90] This is the World to Come.

Points for Discussion

1.   What is the main good and evil involved in reward and punishment? Where is it defined?

2.   Where is the main place of reward and punishment?

3.   Why do we sometimes see good people suffering and evil people prospering?

4.   Why does God reward good? Why does He punish evil?

5.   What is the World to Come?

6.   How is this principle related to that of the immortality of the soul?

בֶּאֱמוּנָה שְׁלֵמָה
בְּבִיאַת הַמָּשִׁיחַ;
וְאַף עַל פִּי שֶׁיִּתְמַהְמֵהַּ,
עִם כָּל־זֶה אֲחַכֶּה־לּוֹ
בְּכָל־יוֹם שֶׁיָּבוֹא.

The Twelfth Principle

I believe with perfect faith in the coming of the Messiah. No matter how long it takes, I will await his coming day.

Yigdal

He will send our Messiah at the End of Days,
To redeem those who await His final salvation.

Commentary on Mishnah

The twelfth principle involves the Messianic Age.

We believe and are certain that the Messiah will come. We do not consider him late, and "although he tarry, we await him."[91]

We should not set a time for his coming, not try to calculate when he will come from scriptural passages. Our sages thus teach us, "May the spirit of those who try to calculate the time of the end rot."[92]

We believe that the Messiah will be greater than any other king or ruler who has ever lived. This has been predicted by every prophet from Moses to Malachi.

One who doubts or minimizes this, denies the Torah itself. For the Messiah is mentioned both in the account of Balaam[93] and at the end of Deuteronomy.[94]

Included in this principle is the belief that a Jewish king can only come from the family of David through his son Solomon. One who rejects this family denies God and His prophets.

Commentary on Sanhedrin 10:1

The Messianic age is when the Jews will regain their independence and all return to the land of Israel.

The Messiah will be a very great king, whose government will be in Zion. He will achieve great fame, and his reputation among the nations will be even greater than that of King Solomon. His great righteousness and the wonders that he will bring about will cause all peoples to make peace with him and all lands to serve him. Whoever rises up against him will be destroyed by God and given over into his hand.

All the Biblical passages that speak of the Messiah thus testify to his success, and to our prosperity that will accompany it.

Nothing will change in the Messianic Age, however, except that the Jews will regain their independence. Our sages thus teach us, "There is no difference between this world and the Messianic Age, except with regard to our subjugation by other governments."[95]

Rich and poor, strong and weak, will still exist in the Messianic Age. It will be very easy for people to make a living, however, and with very little effort they will be able to accomplish very much. This is what our sages mean when they teach us, "In the Future, the land of Israel will bring forth white bread and cloaks of fine wool."[96] This saying is very much like the common expression that people use when someone finds something all prepared and they say, "he has found baked bread and cooked food." Agriculture and harvest will still exist, however, even in the Messianic Age, as the scripture clearly says (*Isaiah 61:3*), "Aliens shall be your plowmen and your vinedressers."

It is for this reason that the sage [who said that Israel will bring forth white bread] became angry at one of his disciples, who took this statement literally. [He answered that we indeed find similar things, even now in this world.] But even this answer, however, was given in the context of the disciple's misunderstanding, and was not the actual truth. We see that this is so, since the Talmud uses this as an example of the teaching (*Proverbs 23:4*), "Do not answer a fool according to his folly."

The main benefit of the Messianic Age will be that we will no longer be under the subjugation of foreign governments who prevent us from keeping all the commandments. It will be a time when the number of wise men will increase, as we find (*Isaiah 11:9*), "All the world will be filled with knowledge." War will no longer exist, as the prophet said (*Ibid. 2:4*), "nation shall no longer lift up sword against nation." It will be an age of great perfection, through which we will become worthy to enter into the World to Come.

The Messiah will then die, and his son will rule in his place.[97] He, in turn, will be followed by *his* son. The Prophet speaks of the Messiah's death when he says (*Isaiah 42:4*), "He shall not fail nor be crushed until he has set right in the world."

His kingdom, however, will last for a very long time. This is because man's lifetime will be vastly extended. Worries and troubles will no longer exist, and therefore people will live much longer. We should therefore not be surprised that the Messiah's kingdom will last for thousands of years.[98] Our sages thus teach us that when this good is brought together, it will not be quickly dispersed.

We do not hope and long for the Messianic Age in order that we might have much grain and wealth. We do not want it so that we should be able to ride horses and indulge in wine and song, as those with confused ideas believe.

The main reason why our prophets and saints have desired the Messianic Age with such a great longing is because it will be highlighted by a community of the righteous and dominated by goodness and wisdom. It will be ruled by [the Messiah, who will be] a righteous and honest king, outstanding in wisdom, and close to God. The scripture therefore says of him (*Psalm 2:7*), "God has said to him, you are My son, I have given birth to you today."

The people in that Age will obey all the commandments of the Torah without neglect or laziness, and nothing will hold them back. This is what the prophet predicted (*Jeremiah 31:34*), "Man will no longer teach his friend and his brother saying, 'know God.' For all of them will know Me, great and small alike." The scripture [speaking of the knowledge of God that comes through the Torah, as the previous verse] says (*Ibid. 31:33*), "I will place My Torah in their hearts."[99] The Prophet likewise said in God's name (*Ezekiel 36:26*), "I will remove the heart of stone from your flesh..." There are many other similar passages that speak along these lines.

It is through this that we will be worthy of the World to Come, which is the final goal...

Code, Repentance
(Yad, Tshuvah)

9:2 All Jews, including their prophets and sages, [have always] longed for the Messianic Age because they wanted relief from the oppressive governments which would not let them observe the Torah and its commandments properly. They wanted to find the tranquility to grow in wisdom, and thus become worthy of life in the World to Come.

The Messianic Age, on the other hand, will be part of our present world. The world will follow its present course with the one exception that the Jews will regain their total independence. Our sages thus teach us, "There is no difference between this world and the Messianic Age, except with regard to our subjugation by other governments."[100]

Code, Governments
(Yad, Melachim)

11:1 The Messiah will be a king who will restore the kingdom of David to its original state. He will rebuild the Temple (*Bais HaMikdash*), and gather together all Jews, no matter where they are scattered.

All the laws of the Torah will be fulfilled as they were originally. The sacrificial system as well as the practices of the Sabbatical Year (*Shemita*) and the Jubilee (*Yovel*) will all be restored.[101] We will then be able to once again observe all the commandments of the Torah.

A person who does not believe in the Messiah, or does not await his coming, denies the most essential teachings of the prophets. Beyond that, he also denies the teachings of both Moses and the Torah.

The Torah itself testifies to the Messianic promise when it says (*Deuteronomy 30:3-5*), "God will restore your fortunes, have mercy on you, and gather you [again from all the countries where He has scattered you]. If He were to banish you to the ends of the heavens [the Lord your God will gather you, and bring you from there]. The Lord your God will bring you [to the land that your fathers occupied. You will occupy it again, and He will make you even more prosperous and numerous than your fathers]." This passage in the Torah includes everything that was predicted by all the prophets [regarding the Messiah].

In the account of Baalam, we likewise find a prophecy regarding the two Messiahs (or anointed ones). The first one was King David, who liberated the Jews from all their initial oppressors. The second is his descendant, the Messiah, who will liberate all Jews in the end.

This is his prophecy (*Numbers 24:17*):

"I see him, but not now"—King David.

"I behold him, but not near"—the Messiah.

"A star shall come forth from Jacob"—King David.

"A scepter shall arise from Israel"—the Messiah.

"He shall smite the squadrons of Moab"—King David.

We thus find that he (*2 Samuel 8:2*), "smote Moab and measured them with a rope."

"He shall break down the sons of Seth"—the Messiah. We thus find that (*Zechariah 9:10*), "his rule shall be from sea to sea."

"Edom shall be his conquest"—King David. It is thus written (*2 Samuel 8:14*), "all Edom became servants to David."

"And Seir, his enemy, shall be his tribute"—the Messiah. It is thus foretold (*Obadiah 1:21*), "Saviors shall come up on Mount Zion [and judge the mount of Esau, and the kingdom shall become that of God]."

11:2 We find further evidence [in the Torah] from the commandment concerning the Cities of Refuge (*Arey Miklat*).[102] [The Torah thus says (*Deuteronomy 19:8,9*), "When God enlarges your borders...and you shall add three cities." This never took place, but it is certain that God would not give a commandment in vain.[103] [We therefore see that this will have to take place in the Messianic Age].

We do not have to bring any proof, however, that the prophets speak of the Messiah, since all their writings are full of this concept.

11:3 Do not think that the Messiah will have to perform signs and miracles. He will not necessarily change the course of nature, bring the dead back to life, or anything else like that.

We thus find that Rabbi Akiba, the greatest sage of the Mishnah, was willing to accept Ben Kosiba as the Messiah, at least until he was killed because of his sins.[105] It was only when he was killed that they realized that they had been wrong and he was not the true Messiah.

We see, however, that the sages did not ask him for any sign or miracle.

The main thing, however, [is that the Messiah will not change our religion in any way]. The Torah that we now have, with all its laws and commandments, will remain the same forever. Nothing will be added to it nor subtracted from it.

11:4 We may assume that an individual is the Messiah if he fulfills the following conditions:

He must be a ruler, from the house of David, immersed in the Torah and its commandments like David his ancestor. He must also follow both the written and the Oral Torah, lead all Jews back to the Torah, strengthen the observance of its laws, and fight God's battles. If one fulfills these conditions, then we may assume that he is the Messiah.

If he does this successfully, and then rebuilds the Temple (*Bais HaMikdash*) on its original site and gathers all the dispersed Jews, then we may be certain that he is the Messiah.

He will then perfect the entire world and bring all men to serve God in unity. It has thus been predicted (*Zephania 3:9*), "I will then give all peoples a pure tongue, that they may call in the name of God, and all serve Him in one manner."

12:1 Do not think that the ways of the world or the laws of nature will change in the Messianic Age. This is not true. The world will continue as it is.

It is true that the prophet Isaiah predicted (*Isaiah 11:6*), "The wolf shall live with the sheep, the leopard shall lie down with the kid." This, however, is merely an allegory, meaning that the Jews will live safely, even with the wicked nations, who are likened to wolves and leopards. We thus find [that the Prophet says of the nations who will punish Israel] (*Jeremiah 5:6*), "A wolf from the plains shall ravish them, a leopard shall prowl in their cities."

All nations will return to the true religion and will no longer steal or oppress. They will eat that which they have honestly attained, together with Israel. This what the Prophet means when he says (*Isaiah 11:7*), "The lion shall eat hay like the ox."

All prophecies such as these regarding the Messiah are allegorical. Only in the Messianic Age will we know the meaning of each allegory and what it comes to teach us.

12:2   Our sages [provided us with an important rule when they] said, "There is no difference between this world and the Messianic Age, except with regard to our subjection to other governments."[106]

From the simple meaning of a number of prophecies, we see that the Messianic Age will begin with the war of Gog and Magog.[107]

Before this war of Gog and Magog, a prophet will arise to rectify the Jews and prepare their hearts. The Prophet foresaw this when he said [in God's name](*Malachi 3:23*), "Behold, I will send you Elijah the prophet [before the great and terrible day of God]."[108]

This prophet will not come to make the clean unclean or the unclean clean. He will not declare that certain individuals are illegitimate when they have been assumed to be legitimate. Neither will he legitimize those who are assumed to be illegitimate. His only task will be to bring peace to the world.[109] The prophecy thus concludes (*Ibid. 3:24*), "He shall turn the hearts of the fathers to their children."

Others of our sages, however, say that Elijah will come immediately before the Messiah,[110] [after the war of Gog and Magog].

In all cases such as these, no man knows what will happen until the time comes. These things were purposely left ambiguous by the prophets. Our [Talmudic] sages likewise did not have any clear tradition in this area, and could therefore only come to some conclusion by interpreting various Biblical passages. It is for this reason that we find so many opinions regarding these matters.

The main thing to remember, however, is that neither the order in which these things will occur, not their details, are fundamentals of our faith. A person should therefore not involve himself in analyzing these traditions. He should not spend time on the Midrashim which were written about such topics, nor consider them overly important. For these things do not bring one to love or fear God.

One should likewise not attempt to calculate when the Messiah will come. Our sages thus said, "May the soul of those who calculate the end rot."[111] One must hope and believe in general, as we have explained.

12:4 Our sages and prophets did not long for the Messianic Age in order that they might rule the world and dominate the gentiles. They did not desire that the nations should honor them, or that they should be able to eat, drink and be merry.

They only wanted one thing, and that was to be free to involve themselves in the Torah and its wisdom. They wanted nothing to disturb or distract them, in order that they should be able to strive to become worthy of life in the World to Come. This has already been discussed in my code on Repentance.

12:5 In the Messianic Age, there will be neither war nor famine. Jealousy and competition will cease to exist, for all good things will be most plentiful, and all sorts of delicacies will be as common as dust.

The main occupation of humanity will only be to know God. The Jews will therefore become great sages, know many hidden things, and achieve the greatest understanding of God possible for a mortal human being. The Prophet thus predicted (*Isaiah 11:9*), "The earth shall be full of the knowledge of God, as the waters cover the sea."

Points for Discussion

1. Who will the Messiah be?

2. How will we know for sure that he is the Messiah?

3. Will he be a prophet? What consequences will this have?

4. Will he be a greater prophet than Moses? Why?

5. What is the reason for the Messianic Age?

6. Will the Messiah necessarily perform miracles? Why?

7. Will we still observe the Torah when the Messiah comes? Why?

8. Why don't we believe that Jesus was the Messiah?

9. What is the war of Gog and Magog?

10. Why will Elijah come before the Messiah?

11. Do you see any signs that the Messianic Age is approaching?

12. Can the Messiah come miraculously any day?

13. What is the "End of Days?"

בֶּאֱמוּנָה שְׁלֵמָה
שֶׁתִּהְיֶה תְּחִיַּת הַמֵּתִים
בְּעֵת שֶׁיַּעֲלֶה רָצוֹן
מֵאֵת הַבּוֹרֵא,
יִתְבָּרַךְ שְׁמוֹ
וְיִתְעַלֶּה זִכְרוֹ
לָעַד וּלְנֵצַח נְצָחִים.

The Thirteenth Principle

I believe with perfect faith that the dead will be brought back to life when God wills it to happen.

Yigdal

God will bring the dead to life with His great love;
May His glorious name be blessed for all time.

Commentary on Mishnah

The thirteenth principle involves the resurrection of the dead

Commentary on Sanhedrin 10:1

The resurrection of the dead is one of the foundations handed down by Moses. One who does not believe in it cannot be associated with Judaism or its religion.

The resurrection, however, is just for the righteous. The Midrash thus says in *Bereshis Rabbah*, "Rain is for both the wicked and righteous, but the resurrection is only for the righteous."[112] It would be absurd for the wicked to be brought back to life, for even while they are alive, they are considered dead. Our sages teach us, "The wicked are considered dead, even during their lifetimes. But the righteous are considered alive, even after they die."[113]

Code, Repentance
(Yad, Tshuvah)

3:6   These have no portion in the World to Come:...Those who deny the resurrection of the dead...[114]

Discourse on the Resurrection
(Ma'amar Techiyas HaMesim)

The concept of the resurrection is well known among all Jews, and there are none who dispute it. It is mentioned many times in our prayers and homilies, as well as in supplications written by the prophets and sages. Inmumerable references to it may be found in the Talmud and Midrash.

This is its significance:

The body and soul will be reunited once again after they have been separated [by death]. There is no Jew who disputes this, and it cannot be interpreted other than literally. One may not accept the view of any Jew who believes otherwise. For we must understand that even though many other Biblical verses may be interpreted allegorically, this must be taken literally.

The concept of the resurrection, namely that body and soul will be re-united after death, is found in the book of Daniel in such a manner that it cannot be interpreted other than literally. We are told (*Daniel 12:2*), "Many who sleep in the dust shall awaken, some to everlasting life, and some to everlasting shame and reproach." Daniel was likewise told by the angel (*Ibid. 12:13*), "Now go your way to the end and rest, and you shall arise to your destiny at the end of days"...

We also see from many pertinent teachings that the men whose souls have been returned to their bodies will eat, drink, marry, have children, and finally die after living a very long time....[115]

Points for Discussion

1. Exactly what is the resurrection of the dead?

2. How is it related to the concept of the immortality of the soul?

3. Read the 37th chapter of Ezekiel. Did this really happen, or was it merely a vision? How is it related to the final resurrection?

4. What effect would a miracle like the resurrection have on the world? How would the world change? What would it be like afterward?

5. Rambam here writes that the resurrected dead will die once again. Many other sages, however, dispute this, and maintain that they will never die. Discuss the significance of these two opinions.

6. Those who hold that the resurrected dead will not die again maintain that the world of the resurrection will lead directly into the World to Come. The World to Come will then include both body and soul. Why do you think that man must also have a body in order to receive his final reward?

7. The Rambam disputes this view, and maintains that the World to Come is completely spiritual. Why does he reject the other opinion? Discuss both opinions.

8. How do you think the dead will be brought back to life? How about those whose bodies no longer exist? What about someone whose body was completely destroyed?

9. How would you react to coming face to face with someone close to you, whom you knew to have died?

Notes

1. See *Moreh Nevuchim* 2:1. Also see introduction to Part 2, No. 16, *Cf. Or HaShem* 1:1:16, 1:2:23, *Amud HaAwodah, Hakdamah Gedolah* No. 15, 31.
2. Rashi *ad loc.*, however, explains this somewhat differently. Instead of "neither separation nor combination," he would read, "neither direction nor weariness."
3. Also see *Deuteronomy 4:39.*
4. *Exodus 9:3, Deuteronomy 2:15, Joshua 4:24, Judges 2:15, I Samuel 5:6, 5:9, 7:13, 12:15, 2 Kings 3:15, Isaiah 19:16, 25:10, 41:20, 59:1, 66:14, Ezekiel 1:3, 3:22,37:1, 40:1, Job 12:9, Ruth 1:13.*
5. *Deuteronomy 11:12, Zechariah 4:10, Psalm 34:16, Proverbs 5:21, 15:3, 22:12, Cf. Genesis 6:8, 38:7, 38:10, Leviticus 10:19,* etc.
6. *Numbers 11:1, 11:18, I Samuel 8:21.*
7. *Cf. Mechilta,* Rashi, on *Exodus 20:2; Rosh HaShanah 17b.*
8. See *Moreh Nevuchim 1:54, 64.*
9. *Job 4:19.*
10. Enosh was the son of Seth, and the grandson of Adam. It was in his generation that idolatry began. See *Genesis 4:26, Targum J.,* Rashi *ad loc.; Shabbos 118b, Mechilta* on *Exodus 20:3 (67b), Sifri (43)* on *Deuteronomy 11:16; 23:5, Yerushalmi, Shekalim 6:2 (26a).* The question as to whether or not Enosh himself was involved in this idolatry is discussed in detail in the Radal on *Pirkey DeRabbi Eliezer 18:52* and *22:4, note 2.*
11. See *Metzudos,* Abarbanel *ad loc.*
12. *Shabbos 92a, Nedarim 38a, Avos 4:1, Shemonah Perakim 7, Moreh Nevuchim 2:36.*
13. That is, *Pardes* or Paradise. See *Yad Yesodey HaTorah 4:13, Chagigah 14b.*
14. *Cf. Avodah Zarah 20b, Yerushalmi Shabbos 1:3, (8b), Yerushalmi Shekalim 3:3 (14b).*
15. *Genesis 28:12, Bereshis Rabbah 68:19.*
16. *Ezekiel 1:5 ff.*
17. *Jeremiah 1:13.*
18. *Ibid. 1:11.*
19. *Ezekiel 2:9.*
20. *Zechariah 5:6.*
21. Others, however, disagree with the Rambam on this point, and hold that exact words were revealed to the prophet, especially where the prophecies were to be recorded in the Bible. See Rambam on *Numbers 23:5, Kuzari 5:20 (50b),* Sforno on *Numbers 22:38* from *2 Samuel 23:2.*
22. *Shabbos 30b, Pesachim 117a.*
23. *Ibid. Cf. 2 Kings 3:15.*
24. *1 Kings 20:35, 2 Kings 2:3, 2:5, 2:7, 2:15, 4:1, 4:38, 5:22, 6:1, 9:1.* See *Targum ad loc.*
25. *Deuteronomy 17:6, 19:15.*
26. *Cf. Bereshis Rabbah 85:3.*
27. *1 Samuel 9:19 ff.*
28. *Yerushalmi Sanhedrin 11:5 (56b). Cf. Tanchuma VaYera 13.*
29. *Job 2:13, Jonah 4:2. Cf. Exodus 34:6, Numbers 14:18, Psalms 103:8, Nehemiah 9:17.*
30. See *Jonah 3:1.*
31. *2 Kings 20:6, Isaiah 38:5, 2 Chronicles 32:26.*
32. *Berachos 7a.*
33. *Shabbos 55a. Cf. Berachos 4a.*
34. See note 28.
35. *Cf. Yerushalmi Sanhedrin 11:6 (57b).*
36. See Rashi *ad loc.* Also see *Ezekiel 2:5.*

37. Literally, the "father" of all prophets. See *VaYikra Rabbah 1:3*.
38. The Kabbalistic interpretation of the anthropomorphic metaphor. See *Kuzari 4:3 (24b), Kol Yehudah ad loc.*, Ibn Ezra on *Exodus 33:20*.
39. That is *Mareh* and *Machazeh*. We find *Mareh* in *Numbers 12:8, Exodus 3:3, Ezekiel 11:24, 43:3, Daniel 8:27, Numbers 8:4. Machazeh* occurs in *Genesis 15:1, Numbers 24:4, 24:16, Ezekiel 13:7.*
40. *Cf. Sifri (68)*, Rashi *ad loc.* Also see Rashi on *Exodus 33:8, Deuteronomy 34:10.*
41. *Sifra ad loc.*
42. See *Moreh Nevuchim 2:34.*
43. *Shabbos 87a.*
44. *Exodus 14:15 ff.*
45. *Exodus 16.*
46. *Numbers 20:8.*
47. *Numbers 16:32.*
48. *Cf. Job 19:27.*
49. *Exodus 20:15.*
50. *Ibid. 20:18.*
51. See *Exodus 14:31.*
52. *Sanhedrin 90a.*
53. *Sanhedrin 10:1 (90a).*
54. *Bereshis Rabbah 8:7. Cf.Baba Basra 15a, Menachos 30a.*
55. See *Sanhedrin 99b.*
56. *Psalms 19:8.*
57. *Sanhedrin 99a. Cf. Avos 3:11.*
58. See note 53.
59. *Sanhedrin 99a, Yerushalmi Sanhedrin 10:1 (49b).*
60. *Job 11:9.*
61. *Cf. Berachos 5a.*
62. *Devarim Rabbah 9:4, Midrash Tehillim 90:3, Pesikta 31 (197a), Yalkut 1:550, Tosefos, Menachos 30a "MiKan," Rosh, Pesachim 10:13.*
63. *Cf. Eruvin 54b, Sifra (43c)* on *Leviticus 9:1, Sifri* on *Deuteronomy 15.*
64. *Avos 1:1.*
65. *Cf. Shabbos 118b.*
66. This took place in the year 204 C.E. *Kitzur Kelaley HaTalmud* (on *Mavo HaTalmud)* "K'sav."
67. *Cf. Shabbos 6b*, Rashi *ad loc.* "Megillas."
68. That is, the Thirteen Principles of Rabbi Ishmael, brought in the prayer book at the beginning of the morning service. See introduction to *Sifra.*
69. The Rambam holds that it was actually put into writing by Rabbi. Rashi, however, disagrees, and maintains that it was not actually written down until several generations later. See Rashi, *Shabbos 13b "Megillas," Eruvin 62b "KeGon," Baba Metzia 33a "VeAina,"* ibid. *85b "U'Misnisa," Succah 28b "Marki," Taanis 12b "DeKeTani."* Also see *Tosefos Megillah 32a "VeHaShoneh," Sefer Mitzvos Gadol,* Introduction (3a), Negative Commandment 65 (16c), *Tshuvos Tashbatz 1:73, 2:53,* Maharatz Chayos, *Taanis 12b, Succah 50b, Baba Metzia 85b.* For a detailed discussion, see *Iggeres Rav Sherira Gaon* and Maharatz Chayos, *Mavo HaTalmud 33.*
70. The Babylonian Talmud was finally redacted in the year 505 C.E. See note 66.
71. Their followers were known as the Saducees *(Tzadukim)* and Bathusians. See *Avos DeRabbi Nathan 5:2,* Rambam on *Avos 1:3, Chulin 1:2, Yadayim 4:6,* Rashbam, *Baba*

Basra 115b, Aruch *"Basusin."* Cf. *Shabbos 108a*, *Menachos 10:3 (65a)*.

72. A sect that did not believe in the Oral Torah.

73. Cf. *Shabbos 68a,b*.

74. One under constraint is exempt from punishment. See *Baba Kama 28b*, *Yad*, *Yesodey HaTorah 5:4*.

75. *Leviticus 3:17, 10:9, 23:14, 23:31, 23:41, 24:3, Numbers 10:8, 15:5, 18:23*.

76. *Baba Metzia 59a, Temurah 16a; Shabbos 104a, Yoma 80a, Megillah 2b, Yerushalmi Megillah 1:5 (7a), Targum J., Sifra (115d)* on *Leviticus 27:34, Devarim Rabbah 8:6, Ruth Rabbah 4:7*.

77. Cf. *Ezekiel 8:12*.

78. See *Moreh Nevuchim 1:69*.

79. *Ibid. 3:20,21*.

80. *Ibid. 1:68*. Also see *Likutey Amarim (Tanya) 1:2* in *Hagah*, quoting *Pardes Rimonim 8:13*. Cf. *Shiur Komah 13:12*.

81. *Genesis 42:15,16*.

82. *1 Samuel 1:26, 17:55, 20:3, 25:26, 2 Samuel 11:11, 14:19, 2 Kings 2:2, 4:6, 4:30*.

83. Or "as God lives." *Judges 8:19, I Samuel 14:39, 14:45, 19:6, 20:3, 20:21, 25:26, 25:34, 26:10, 26:16, 28:10, 29:6, 2 Samuel 4:9, 12:5, 14:11, 15:21, 22:47, I Kings 1:29, 2:24, 17:1, 17:12, 18:10, 18:15, 22:14, 2 Kings 2:2, 2:4, 2:6, 3:14, 4:30, 5:16, 5:20, Jeremiah 4:2, 5:2, 12:16, 16:14,15, 23:7,8, 38:16, Hoseah 4:15, Psalms 18:47, Ruth 3:13, 2 Chronicles 18:13*.

84. See *Moreh Nevuchim 3:20*.

85. *Job 11:9*.

86. See *Shabbos 32b, 105b, Kesuvos 8b, Sotah 49a, Koheles Rabbah 4:1*. Also see *Sifra (93a,b), Targum J.,*Rashi on *Leviticus 20:20, 20:21, Yevamos 55a, Tosefos, Yevamos 2a "Eshes."*

87. This refers to boys under the age of 13, and girls under 12.

88. *Sifri (280)*, Rashi *ad loc.*, *BeMidbar Rabbah 8:4*.

89. *Avos 4:11*.

90. *Kiddushin 39b, Chulin 142b*.

91. *Habakkuk 2:3*.

92. *Sanhedrin 97b*.

93. *Numbers 24:7*.

94. *Deuteronomy 30:3 ff*.

95. *Berachos 34b, Shabbos 63a, 151b, Pesachim 68a, Sanhedrin 91b, 99a*.

96. *Shabbos 30b*.

97. See Bachya on *Genesis 11:11*, who holds that the Messiah will never die.

98. Cf. *Sanhedrin 99a*.

99. This is the "new covenant" mentioned in *Jeremiah 31:31*. Here we see that this merely refers to the renewed observance of the Torah.

100. See note 95.

101. See *Erchin 32b, Yad, Shemitah VeYovel 12:16*.

102. *Numbers 35:9 ff*.

103. See *Sifri (185) ad loc., Yerushalmi Makkos 3:6 (7b), Yad, Rotzeach 8:4*.

104. *Yerushalmi Taanis 4:5 (24a) Eicha Rabbah 2:4. Cf. Sanhedrin 97b*.

105. In the above sources, we find that Bar Kosiba was killed by an act of God. For a different opinion, see *Sanhedrin 93b*. Ravad, Radbaz, *Kesef Mishneh*, here.

106. See note 95.

107. *Ezekiel 38, 39*. Also see *Berachos 7b, Shabbos 118a, Succah 52b, Megillah 11a,*

Sanhedrin 17a, 97b, Eduyos 2:10, Targum J. on *Exodus 40:10, Numbers 11:26, 24:17, Deuteronomy 32:29,* Radak on *Zechariah 14:1.*

108.   See *Tana Debei Eliahu Rabbah 18 (86b), Yeshuos Yaakov ad loc. 51.* Also see Radal on *Pirkey DeRabbi Eliezer 43:85.*

109.   *Eduyos 8:7.*

110.   *Eruvin 43b, Tosefos ad loc. "DeLo."* Also see *Yad, Nezirus 4:11.*

111.   See note 92.

112.   This is actually found in *Taanis 7a.* A somewhat similar saying occurs in *Bereshis Rabbah 13:6,* but it is not the saying brought here. This saying occurs nowhere in *Bereshis Rabbah.* It is most probable that the Rambam had a different reading in the Midrash.

113.   *Berachos 18b.*

114.   *Sanhedrin 10:1 (90a).*

115.   See *Sanhedrin 92a,b.*